*DIAGNOSING CLASSROOM LEARNING ENVIRONMENTS*

TEACHER RESOURCE BOOKLETS ON CLASSROOM
SOCIAL RELATIONS AND LEARNING

# Diagnosing Classroom Learning Environments

ROBERT FOX
MARGARET BARRON LUSZKI
RICHARD SCHMUCK
*Center for Research on Utilization of Scientific Knowledge*
*Institute for Social Research*
*University of Michigan*

Science Research Associates, Inc.   Chicago

A Subsidiary of IBM

Library of Congress Catalog Card Number: 65-29237

Part of the research reported herein was supported through the Cooperative Research Program of the Office of Education, U.S. Department of Health, Education, and Welfare, under Contract SAE 9159. Under the terms of that contract the federal government has a royalty-free license for the use of the material contained herein that appeared in any reports to the federal government under the above-mentioned contract.

The publisher gratefully acknowledges the copyright holders' permissions to quote and summarize from:
—*Characteristics of School Classroom Environments over Time,* by W. C. Morse, R. Bloom, and J. Dunn. University School Research Project (U.S. Office of Education Grant 04632), School of Education, University of Michigan, Ann Arbor, 1964.
—*Interaction Analysis in the Classroom: A Manual for Observers,* by Ned A. Flanders. Rev. ed. School of Education, University of Michigan, January 1964.
—*Minority Group and Class Status as Related to Social and Personality Factors in Scholastic Achievement,* by Martin Deutsch. (Monograph No. 2.) Ithaca, N.Y.: The Society for Applied Anthropology, 1960.
—"Pupil Perceptions of Parental Attitudes Toward School," by M. B. Luszki and R. Schmuck, *Mental Hygiene,* April 1965.
—*The Self Concepts of Elementary School Children in Relation to Their Academic Achievement, Intelligence, Interests and Manifest Anxiety,* by J. C. Bledsoe and K. C. Garrison. Copyright 1962, the University of Georgia College of Education. By permission of J. C. Bledsoe, K. C. Garrison, and the University of Georgia.
—"Validation of the Incomplete Sentences Test of School Adjustment," by Leslie F. Malpass and Forrest B. Tyler. Unpublished paper, Southern Illinois University, 1961.

# PREFACE

The teacher who wants to keep abreast of the new knowledge in the behavioral sciences and utilize it to improve his teaching techniques and professional effectiveness faces a formidable challenge. Fortunately this challenge is not solely the teacher's responsibility. Scientists from the various disciplines are seeking ways of collaborating with educational specialists to apply developments in the behavioral sciences to the classroom and to improve channels of communication to teachers.

*Diagnosing Classroom Learning Environments* is one of the three TEACHER RESOURCE BOOKLETS ON CLASSROOM SOCIAL RELATIONS AND LEARNING that grew out of such a cooperative research effort. At the Center for Research on Utilization of Scientific Knowledge at the University of Michigan, a team of social scientists and educational specialists for over a decade has been exploring some of the possibilities for cooperative research in the behavioral sciences and the application of the results of such research to the classroom. The projects have been supported by the U.S. Office of Education,[1] the National Institute of Mental Health,[2] and the McGregor Foundation.

The relation between classroom interpersonal relations and the effective learning of subject matter has been investigated through research questions such as these: What effect does the social power or social acceptance possessed or lacked by students have on their learning? What are the dynamics that make it difficult for a socially ineffective child to improve his status in the group? What kinds of perceptions and expectations do teachers and students have of one another? What are the effects of children of different ages learning together? How can the socially ineffective child be helped to use his learning potential better?

Data have been gathered from several hundred classrooms through the use of diagnostic tools dealing with classroom social structures; individual and group attitudes toward learning; significant environmental forces influencing both teachers and students; and the nature of the student-teacher interaction. On the basis of these data the teachers participating in the research projects modified many of the preliminary diagnostic instruments and developed plans for altering their teaching methods to improve the learning climate of the classroom. Much ingenuity was shown by the participating teachers in taking the step from "What do the data say?" to "What can be done in my classroom to improve mental health and learn-

---

[1] OE contract SAE 9159.
[2] NIMH grants M 919, OM 376, MH 0170-08.

ing?" Further data were then gathered, again through the use of diagnostic tools, on the success or failure of the various plans and teaching methods that were developed.

This series of TEACHER RESOURCE BOOKLETS ON CLASSROOM SOCIAL RELATIONS AND LEARNING will present some of the knowledge gained from those studies.

*Problem Solving to Improve Classroom Learning* is the most comprehensive of the three booklets. It describes the whole problem-solving sequence, from perception of classroom difficulties through the evaluation of the remedial action taken. It deals with the issues of identifying problems in classroom life; selecting or developing appropriate diagnostic tools to analyze these problems; using diagnostic data and behavioral science resources to develop a plan for improving the learning atmosphere in the classroom; carrying out planned changes in classroom life; and evaluating the changes. Practical illustrations are provided from the experience of a variety of teachers and students who participated in the research projects.

*Diagnosing Classroom Learning Environments* focuses upon one stage of the problem-solving sequence—the process of getting reliable information about the actual state of affairs in the classroom. It presents and discusses some of the data-gathering instruments and techniques that have proved useful; it also provides suggestions on organizing the data so that the teacher can focus his efforts to change the classroom learning environment.

*Role-Playing Methods in the Classroom* is about a technique that has proved useful to many teachers for dealing with a variety of classroom problems and reaching certain learning objectives. The booklet discusses the theoretical background of role playing and gives a step-by-step discussion of how to use role playing in the classroom. There are sample role-playing situations; suggestions on how to get started; advice on when to be cautious; discussions of the appropriateness of role playing for children of various ages and backgrounds; and case studies of groups of teachers and students using role playing under a variety of circumstances and for a variety of reasons.

The three booklets were written to complement each other. Since *Problem Solving* describes the whole problem-solving sequence in the classroom, it would be advantageous to read it first. It will provide an overview of the series and give the general framework of processes and concepts into which the other two booklets fit. However, although it describes a variety of methods designed to improve the classroom learning atmosphere, it does not do so with the extensive discussion and wealth of illustrative material that is focused upon one such method in *Role-Playing Methods*. And although *Role-Playing Methods* describes in detail one way of working with classroom problems, it has no extended treatment of how these problems are analyzed, of how data are gathered about the problems, or of how progress is to be measured. For a detailed analysis of problem-discovery and data-gathering techniques, the reader is referred to *Diagnosing Classroom Learning Environments.*

The reader who wants to examine the theories and the research findings on which these three booklets are based is advised to turn to *Understanding Classroom Social Relations and Learning.*[3] The theories that relate classroom interpersonal relations and subject-matter learning are fully elaborated in that book, and the results of ten years of research in the schools to investigate the validity of these theories are presented.

The degree to which the school should be allowed to inquire into the personal and interpersonal life of the student is occasionally questioned. Articles have been written about the dangers of psychological tests, and legislation has been introduced in some states to restrict or prevent teachers and scientists from obtaining and utilizing such information. This matter is of fundamental concern to teachers who would act upon the suggestions in this series of booklets.

The research findings described in *Understanding Classroom Social Relations and Learning* give major support to the desirability of vigorous efforts on the part of the school and the teacher to understand and improve the mental health and learning climate of the classroom. The research has found that the mentally healthy student does learn academic subject matter better. Teachers who can diagnose and improve the learning atmosphere of their classroom can thereby be better teachers. Accordingly, the teaching profession would be wise to extend its understanding of classroom social procedures and the techniques for dealing with them, while at the same time exercising caution so that the use of these techniques is not extended beyond the teacher's competence and the limits of the educational environment.

Unprofessional use of information about students and unwise applications of diagnostic data by teachers can be greatly reduced by better teacher training, by providing more focused and usable diagnostic materials, and by opening the channels of communication between the social scientist and the teacher. The materials in this series of booklets and the research on which they are based are directed toward these goals.

We wish to acknowledge the extensive teamwork that has made these research projects possible. In addition to the coauthors of this booklet, Robert Fox, Margaret Barron Luszki, and Richard Schmuck, other senior collaborators in the projects have been Mark Chesler, Mabel Kaufman,

---

[3]R. Fox, R. Lippitt, R. Schmuck, and E. Van Egmond (Chicago: Science Research Associates, 1966).

Ronald Lippitt, and Elmer Van Egmond. The secretarial work has been led with dedication by Karen Donahue. If it were possible, each classroom teacher, each principal, each interviewer, each statistician, and each social scientist who made his unique contribution would be introduced to the reader by name. That so many should become so highly involved in an effort requiring extensive time beyond the usual demands and professional skill beyond that normally expected speaks well of their concern for the ideas presented in this series of booklets. We hope their efforts are rewarded by your finding *Diagnosing Classroom Learning Environments* truly helpful.

RONALD LIPPITT
ROBERT FOX
*Program Coordinators*

# TABLE OF CONTENTS

# A LIST OF DIAGNOSTIC TOOLS

# CHAPTER ONE

# *Introduction*

Classroom interaction is more than a matter of the teacher telling and the pupils listening or of the teacher asking and the pupils answering. Learning does not occur merely because of the teacher's presentations; it occurs through the interplay of the teacher's behavior with many other forces.

Teachers and others sophisticated in concepts of mental health know the important relation between personality and social factors on the one hand and utilization of intellectual potential on the other. They realize that when the pupil arrives at school he already has certain personality characteristics that will affect his behavior in the classroom and his motivation to participate in learning activities. He brings to the classroom feelings about academic achievement and a concept of himself as a pupil. Some pupils bring tendencies toward independence, others toward dependence; some are friendly, others hostile or defensive; some are expressive and charming, others introverted or even withdrawn.

Teachers are generally aware that the attitudes of family members and other persons in the child's environment have been critical in shaping these characteristics during his preschool years, and that these external influences will continue throughout his school years. In each classroom as well, complex patterns of social and psychological relations operate constantly, creating a classroom learning climate that can significantly affect a pupil's academic motivation.

If the schools are to help our children maximize their abilities and become effective citizens, teachers must know more about their pupils than their current IQs and their achievement levels in various academic areas. Although the teacher may not be able fully to control all the attitudes and relations that influence his pupils and the classroom climate, he should

1

be able to identify and to understand them. Also, if he is to create and maintain a classroom environment that supports learning, he should plan and execute ways of modifying them.

The purpose of this booklet is to help teachers achieve such knowledge and understanding. It makes available those instruments that have proved useful in diagnosing some of the important social and psychological factors inherent in the classroom learning atmosphere, and it describes some ways in which the information obtained can be recorded, interpreted, and acted upon. It is closely related to a companion booklet, *Problem Solving to Improve Classroom Learning,*[1] which describes a problem-solving sequence that includes (1) identifying classroom problems, (2) diagnosing and interpreting them, (3) developing and carrying out plans for change, and (4) evaluating such changes. The diagnostic tools presented here are parts of that broader framework. They provide a simple and relatively objective way to identify problems, they help the teacher diagnose a specific problem and interpret its meaning, and they provide a sound basis on which to develop a plan for change. Finally, they facilitate evaluation of the change to determine its effectiveness.

These tools can enhance a teacher's understanding of his classroom. They permit him to view, from various perspectives, the complex forces operating in the classroom—attitudes that pupils bring into the classroom as a result of outside forces, feelings between individual pupils and among subgroups in the classroom, reactions to different aspects of the teacher's behavior and to specific learning experiences. The teacher can use this information to improve the learning atmosphere in his classroom. Generally he can do this without seeking outside help, though it may often be useful to discuss his findings and plans with an interested colleague who is also using the tools or with his principal or supervisor.

Occasionally some of these tools suggest another kind of problem: they may identify an individual child who appears to be poorly adjusted in the classroom group. Although teachers can do much to help and support such children, often the special knowledge of a trained counselor or psychologist is needed. Teachers are urged to seek such aid as soon as there is an indication that it may be needed.

Each of the tools in this pamphlet is important in its own right and can be used independently for a specific purpose. But the factors involved in classroom interaction are often much better understood if they are analyzed from more than one point of view. The data derived from one instrument may be interpreted far more meaningfully when compared with those from one or more other instruments, and such comparison may give

---

[1] R. Schmuck, M. Chesler, and R. Lippitt (Chicago: Science Research Associates, 1966).

the teacher a clearer indication of the desirable courses of action. The authors suggest that the teacher develop a package of appropriate tools for use in a particular situation.

Thus as he reads about the tools in the separate chapters, the teacher should keep in mind that they represent related areas of concern. To convey this overall picture, the following section of this chapter, A Survey of the Diagnostic Tools, will give a brief but comprehensive preview of all the diagnostic materials presented in Chapters Two through Nine. The final section, Classroom Diagnosis and Educational Objectives, describes briefly the relation of these tools to each other and to the school curriculum as a whole. It also presents several notes of caution for a teacher who is contemplating a diagnostic program for his classroom. In Chapter Ten, "Planning and Accomplishing Classroom Diagnosis," a hypothetical calendar of tools is outlined and consideration given to the selection and use of tools to meet the needs of particular classrooms. Finally, three case studies are presented to show how the tools have been used in solving specific classroom problems.

## A Survey of the Diagnostic Tools

In this survey the theoretical premises of each chapter are stated, followed by the overall objective of that chapter and a synopsis of each of the diagnostic tools that have proved useful in reaching these objectives. Additional material presented in the chapters, such as case studies and methods of tabulating and analyzing pupil responses to the tools, has been omitted from this survey.

### Chapter Two—Assessing the Classroom Learning Climate

*Premises:* Many factors within the classroom environment can affect a pupil's motivation to learn. The teacher can help pupils learn their academic subjects better when he takes some of these factors into account.

*Objective:* To help the teacher see which factors are affecting his classroom's learning atmosphere—and how—so that he may direct his efforts to encouraging pupils to improve their academic motivations.

*Diagnostic Tools:*

1. *Classroom Life.* To obtain a general view of the classroom learning climate: How do the pupils feel about the class? How interested and diligent do they see themselves as pupils? How attracted are they to schoolwork, teachers, and one another?

2. *My Teacher.* To see how pupils would like the teacher to change: To what degree—more, less, or the same as now—should he help them with work, make sure work is done, trust them on their own, or make them work hard?

3

3. *Clues About Classroom Life.* To obtain specific information about the classroom learning climate: What do the pupils feel are clues to "good" and "bad" days, and what would they like to see happen oftener in the classroom?

4. *Postclass Reactions.* To obtain pupil reactions to learning experiences soon after they have taken place: What feelings did the pupils have about the learning activities? Was the content clear and interesting? Did the pupil think he or other pupils needed special help?

### Chapter Three—Social Relations in the Classroom

*Premises:* The patterns of social relations within a classroom are apt to affect a pupil's utilization of his academic potential. The teacher can work more easily and effectively when each pupil has positive relations with some peers in the classroom.

*Objective:* To help the teacher analyze these patterns so that he can initiate changes that allow more pupils to have positive relations with peers.

*Diagnostic Tools:*

5. *How I Feel About Others in My Class.* To determine the friendship patterns in the class: Are some pupils very popular with their peers, some unpopular, some relatively or totally neglected; or are the likes and dislikes more evenly distributed?

6. *The People in My Class.* To see how pupils evaluate each other in terms of social and learning objectives: Which pupils are seen by their peers as the class leaders in influence, as cooperating best with the teacher, as capable of academic improvement, and as learning best?

### Chapter Four—Pupil Norms in Classroom Life

*Premises:* Pupils can form group standards of classroom activities that affect the academic involvement of individual pupils. These group standards can be used to facilitate academic learning if the teacher is able to work with them.

*Objective:* To help the teacher analyze these pupil norms so that he can act to influence norms that are not supporting academic ends.

*Diagnostic Tools:*

7. *How This Class Feels.* To measure how pupils perceive their peers' attitudes: How do they think their peers react to issues such as classroom participation, asking the teacher for help, and helping peers with work?

8. *How Do You Feel About These Things?* To measure the individual pupils' standards in regard to these classroom issues.

9. *How Do You Think Your Teacher Feels?* To measure how the pupils perceive the teacher's expectations.

### Chapter Five—Pupil-Teacher Interaction

*Premises:* The teacher's behavior in the classroom is influential in determining how pupils will respond to academic experiences. He can reach his educational objectives more efficiently if he is aware of the effects of his interactions with pupils.

*Objective:* To help the teacher compare his educational objectives and intended teaching methods with the actual classroom interaction that his behavior produces.

*Diagnostic Tools:*

10. *Pupil Perceptions of a Class Period.* To establish how pupils see classroom interaction during part of a school day: How much and what kind of talking did the teacher and the pupils do? What were the pupils' feelings about their interaction with the teacher?

11 and 12. *Classroom Observation Schedules.* To establish the origin, content, and direction of teacher and pupil behaviors: Is the teacher's behavior aimed at the whole class or at individual pupils? Are teacher and pupil actions oriented to work or to social behavior and control?

13. *Outline of Interaction Analysis.* To measure the teacher's influence patterns: Is teacher behavior mainly direct or indirect? What proportion of time does the teacher lecture, praise, or ask questions? What are the pupils' responses to different types of teacher influence?

### Chapter Six—Outside Influences on Pupil Learning

*Premises:* Many forces outside the classroom impinge on pupils' lives to affect their school achievement and behavior. The teacher can make classroom experiences more important and meaningful for the pupils if he understands these forces.

*Objective:* To provide the teacher with insight into the nature and working of these forces so that he may provide classroom experiences to compensate for those that do not support learning.

*Diagnostic Tools:*

14. *Getting Acquainted with You.* To obtain information on a pupil's home and educational background: Does the pupil have brothers and sisters? What are their ages? Where was the pupil's previous schooling? Does he have a part-time job?

15. *Parts of Your Day.* To establish how important the different parts of a pupil's day are for him: How important is life in this

class in relation to the other parts of the day?

16. *Changing the Parts of Your Day.* To establish how the pupil would like to change the amount of time he spends in each part of his day: Does the pupil want to spend more or less time in class?

17. *Talking with People.* To establish what people the pupil considers important in his life: How important is the pupil's teacher in comparison with other people?

18. *How Satisfied Are They?* To measure the pupil's perceptions of other people's feelings about his schoolwork: How do the pupil's ideas of his teacher's satisfactions and the satisfactions of his parents and peers compare?

19. *How They See Me.* To measure the pupil's perceptions of the other people's evaluations of him: How do the pupil's perceptions of his teacher's and principal's evaluations of him compare with his perceptions of his friends' and parents' evaluations?

## Chapter Seven—Parental Influences on School Adjustment

*Premises:* His parents' attitudes toward school and the way he perceives these attitudes will affect a pupil's academic achievement. The teacher can improve a pupil's classroom experiences when he has information about parental attitudes and home climate and about how the pupil perceives these influences on him.

*Objective:* To help the teacher analyze the congruence as well as the effects of these attitudes and perceptions so that he can take them into account in planning classroom learning experiences.

*Diagnostic Tools:*

14. *Getting Acquainted with You* (continued from Chapter Six). To obtain information on a pupil's parents, their occupations, and their education. (Other methods of evaluation are suggested, such as pupil essays. See also Tools 22 and 23 in Chapter Nine.)

## Chapter Eight—The Pupil's Concept of Himself

*Premises:* The level of a pupil's self-esteem can be a significant factor in determining how he utilizes his academic potential. The teacher can facilitate a pupil's motivation and academic learning by enhancing his self-esteem.

*Objective:* To help the teacher analyze the pupil's view of himself so that he can plan classroom experiences that will affect the self-concept in a positive way.

*Diagnostic Tools:*

20. *My Classmates.* To see how the pupil evaluates himself in relation to his classmates: How positively or negatively does the

pupil think of himself in comparison with his peers? (See also Tools 22 and 23 in Chapter Nine.)

21. *Self-Concept Scale.* To compare those qualities a pupil attributes to himself with those he wishes he could attribute to himself.

## Chapter Nine—Sentence Completions: A Multidimensional Diagnostic Tool

*Premises:* What a pupil writes in completing specially designed unfinished sentences is often a very personal expression of his attitudes toward many aspects of his life. The teacher can derive considerable insight into these feelings by allowing for such expression.

*Objective:* To provide the teacher with the means of eliciting such expressions and interpreting them in relation to the broad range of academic and social objectives described in the preceding chapters.

*Diagnostic Tools:*

22. *Sentence-Completion Form.* To establish how the pupil perceives his teacher, schoolwork, peers, parents, and self by his completions of open-ended sentences.

23. *Multiple-Choice Sentence-Completion Form.* To measure how the pupil perceives various aspects of his school life by his selection of one of several possible completions for an incomplete sentence.

## *Classroom Diagnosis and Educational Objectives*

The many factors that interact to produce a particular classroom climate have characteristics similar to the complex, delicate balance of a physiological system. A doctor, in diagnosing a patient's illness, selects from among the many available tests and laboratory procedures the few that are relevant to that patient's history and complaints. He rarely selects only one, for he must integrate data of many kinds into his diagnosis. In the same way a teacher, on the basis of his knowledge and experience of his class, will inevitably feel that certain of the tools described above are more relevant than others to the ages and backgrounds of his pupils and the problems and characteristics of his class. Some guidelines for developing an appropriate tool kit will be found in Chapter Ten.

After suitable tools are selected, other questions arise. For the teacher who is using such a tool for the first time, a major question is how to introduce it to his pupils. There is no magic formula, no one correct procedure for introducing this type of test and putting pupils at ease in using it: each group of pupils and each tool will require unique handling. The teacher's experience and personality are additional factors that contribute to determining the most appropriate procedure. If the teacher is able to convey to the children the attitude that these tools are a routine part of the classroom activity, it will help to put them in a relaxed mood. He will ease his own anxieties about those tools which give students the opportunity to be critical of him if he recognizes that only when these negative feelings have been brought out can he deal with them in any effective way or attempt to turn them in a positive direction.

An almost necessary step is to have the pupils use numbers rather than their names on the forms they fill in. These numbers, which should not follow alphabetical name sequence, can be assigned privately at the start of the year's testing program. Many teachers may feel that pupils will respond to the tools more freely and frankly if they can respond anonymously. This feeling is valid in some instances, but it must be weighed against the fact that maximum utilization of the tools is possible only when a problem group can be pinpointed or a troubled child identified for professional help. Data from certain of the tools would be meaningless under conditions of anonymity. Suggestions for administration are given in the early chapters, and problems of anonymity are considered wherever they are especially relevant.

A final caution: Teachers who use these diagnostic tools should be aware that there are recurrent public objections to "invasion of privacy" of pupils and their families. Some public efforts have been made to restrict sociometric and psychological testing and questioning in the public schools; some have succeeded. Like all complex tools, the tests in this pamphlet must be used with skill and understanding. Teachers who use them have an ethical responsibility to guard and respect the confidential personal and family information obtained from students. Like the physician who has taken the Hippocratic oath, the teacher must use such information to benefit only those he serves, and he should obtain only that information which is likely to enhance the student's learning experience and personal development. Furthermore, he will be wise to employ the tools only with the approval and confidence of his principal and be prepared to explain his objectives and methods and to show his peers and his pupils' parents how findings would be used.

Some action plans based on the tools are presented for illustrative purposes, particularly in the case studies. In general, however, this is a booklet of tools that are most effectively used as implements in a broader plan of classroom study and action. Teachers are urged to refer to a companion booklet of this series, *Problem Solving to Improve Classroom Learning,* for help in selecting tools appropriate to their particular situation, for interpretation of the full meaning of their findings, and for guidance in developing plans for any changes that may be indicated.

# CHAPTER TWO

# Assessing the Classroom Learning Climate

The way a pupil feels about his peers, about his studies, and about his teacher is one of the major factors determining how much he will benefit from his classroom experience. A classroom learning atmosphere that provides emotional support, encouragement, and mutual respect is conducive to high self-esteem and to the utilization of academic abilities. Without supportive classroom relationships, pupils often lack interest in learning, and the dual educational goals of academic learning and mental health are difficult to achieve.

Both experience and research show that pupils tend to respond favorably to the learning situation when the teacher presents his methods and objectives to them clearly and concretely, when he makes frequent checks of their reactions to classroom activities, and when he takes their points of view into consideration. Pupils who misperceive the teacher's intentions or who cannot find expression for their interests in academic procedures often fail to become involved in the learning process and to utilize their intellectual potentials.

## Measuring the Learning Atmosphere

Teachers traditionally use quizzes, tests, or recitations to measure what has been learned during a specific teaching-learning sequence. These devices inevitably leave certain basic questions unanswered or create such new ones as these:

9

⚡ • Did the pupils feel free to participate in the learning activity?
• Was it clear to them why we did that activity?
• How many of them felt lost because of the rate at which we moved?
• Who felt, but didn't express, the need for extra help?

These and other questions about a pupil's reactions to his academic experience can be answered by two analogous types of diagnostic measurement, direct and indirect. Both types can be used to measure a pupil's perceptions of his own motivations to learn, of the classroom learning climate and his involvement in it, or of a lesson he has recently had. Many other pertinent aspects of pupil reaction to learning situations can be diagnosed by the tools described in Chapter Five, which focuses on pupil-teacher interaction.

Direct measurement uses either multiple-choice endings for an incomplete sentence, such as 'When I'm in this class, I . . . " or multiple-choice answers to direct questions, such as "How often do the pupils in this class help one another with their schoolwork?" Responses to this type can be scored rapidly and interpreted easily.

Indirect measurement uses open-ended sentences, such as "When I'm in this class, I _____," for which the pupil composes an ending in his own words instead of selecting one of several alternative endings. The responses require more subtle, qualitative scoring and interpretation, but are frequently very rich and meaningful. A multipurpose sentence-completion tool and its analysis are described fully in Chapter Nine; the present chapter considers those items in the tool that are especially pertinent to pupil reactions to learning experience.

Since certain items in the following tools allow for responses that are critical of the teacher or his methods, pupil anonymity may result in more freedom of response. Where questions concern the teacher or classroom learning experiences, some teachers have appointed a committee of respected pupil leaders to collect, tabulate, and report the overall class response. Particularly where criticism of the teacher is involved, pupils are more free to express their feelings to their peers than to the teacher. Such anonymity, however, results in the loss of valuable data, and the preferred procedure is for teachers to try to allay fears of reprisal for frank replies. By showing that they will be objective about the results and genuinely interested in doing something about them, many teachers have encouraged their pupils to be frank and to use this opportunity constructively.

### Measuring General Learning Experiences

Tool 1, Classroom Life, designed to give the teacher a general view of his classroom climate, can be administered in from five to ten minutes and the forms from the whole class can be scored in fifteen.

The content of this form—and of all others in this booklet—is primarily suggestive. Although the directions, questions, and alternative responses can be used effectively in most classrooms, a teacher may wish to design a questionnaire that reflects his specific concerns with his own class and the special needs of his pupils.

Several techniques may facilitate the physical administration of this and most other diagnostic tools. If the pupils can read the form themselves, the teacher needs only to give brief directions before asking them to fill it out honestly and quickly. If the pupils cannot read very well, the teacher may have them choose their answers after he has read each item aloud. The pupils should be seated so as to permit maximum privacy. The teacher should also work out some procedure for collecting the sheets or having them dropped in a box on his desk, rather than having them passed forward in customary fashion. Finally, the teacher should remind the class to write in the date, their assigned numbers, and the class on each form.

The responses to these nine items can be tabulated easily. A piece of paper can be divided into six columns, for choices a through f, and nine horizontal rows; the separate tallies will be entered in the appropriate

## TOOL 1

```
                                    Date _____

                                    Your number _____

                                    Class _____
```

CLASSROOM LIFE

Here is a list of some statements that describe life in the classroom. Circle the letter in front of the statement that best tells how you feel about this class. There are no right or wrong answers.

1. Life in this class with your regular teacher has

    a.  all good things

    b.  mostly good things

    c.  more good things than bad

    d.  about as many good things as bad

    e.  more bad things than good

    f.  mostly bad things

2. How hard are you working these days on learning what is being taught at school?

    a. Very hard.

    b. Quite hard.

    c. Not very hard.

    d. Not hard at all.

3. When I'm in this class, I

    a. usually feel wide awake and very interested

    b. am pretty interested, kind of bored part of the time

    c. am not very interested, bored quite a lot of the time

    d. don't like it, feel bored and not with it

4. How hard are you working on schoolwork compared with the others in the class?

    a. Harder than most.

    b. A little harder than most.

    c. About the same as most.

    d. A little less than most.

    e. Quite a bit less than most.

5. How many of the pupils in this class do what the teacher suggests?

    a. Most of them do.

    b. More than half do.

    c. Less than half do.

    d. Hardly anybody does.

6. If we help each other with our work in this class, the teacher

    a. likes it a lot

    b. likes it some

    c. likes it a little

    d. doesn't like it at all

---

7.  How good is your schoolwork compared with the work of others in the class?

    a.  Much better than most.

    b.  A little better than most.

    c.  About the same as most.

    d.  Not quite as good as most.

    e.  Much worse than most.

8.  How often do the pupils in this class help one another with their schoolwork?

    a.  Most of the time.

    b.  Sometimes.

    c.  Hardly ever.

    d.  Never.

9.  How often do the pupils in this class act friendly toward one another?

    a.  Always.

    b.  Most of the time.

    c.  Sometimes.

    d.  Hardly ever.

---

squares. The teacher will want to inspect both the responses of the entire classroom, shown on this tally sheet, and those of subgroups or individuals who deviate from the rest of the class, shown on individual answer sheets.

Tool 2, which teachers have found of significant assistance, permits pupils to register their feelings about certain of the teacher's characteristics and classroom methods. Since the teacher would probably consider only those changes favored by a substantial number of pupils within the classroom, rather than by only a few individuals, anonymity is desirable because of the very personal nature of the responses.

Each teacher will probably have greater interest in certain of the items in these two instruments than in others. If, for example, he has been planning classroom cooperation through peer tutoring and small study groups but finds that his pupils feel he does not approve of their mutual assistance, he will see where he must communicate his intentions

13

more clearly. Also, from each pupil's comparison of himself with others in Tool 1, the teacher can see which pupils misjudge their academic skills and need help in correcting their inaccurate self-perceptions as pupils. Such comparisons cannot be made, of course, if this tool has been filled out anonymously.

A choice made from among the alternative answers to an item such as "Life in this class with your regular teacher has . . ." from Tool 1

## TOOL 2

Date _____

Class _____

(Don't write your number.)

MY TEACHER

Pretend that you could have your teacher change in some way. For each number, check the box that best tells how you would like your teacher to act in this class. There are no right or wrong answers.

| | Much more than he does now | A little more than he does now | The same as he does now | A little less than he does now | Much less than he does now |
|---|---|---|---|---|---|
| 1. Help with work | | | | | |
| 2. Yell at us | | | | | |
| 3. Make sure work is done | | | | | |
| 4. Ask us to decide about how we will work | | | | | |
| 5. Smile and laugh | | | | | |
| 6. Make us behave | | | | | |
| 7. Trust us on our own | | | | | |
| 8. Make us work hard | | | | | |
| 9. Show that he understands how we feel | | | | | |

will be a general answer, fully meaningful to the teacher only when supported by additional information. Open-ended questions can produce this information. By completing sentences like "Some of the best things about this class are _____" and "Some of the worst things about this class are _____," pupils can provide some extremely incisive criticisms of classroom life, both positive and negative.

Other open-ended items can assist the teacher in diagnosing individual reactions to academic matters. The following five sentences were completed respectively by a pupil with a high attraction to school and a pupil very alienated from school.

Studying is (*a chance to learn what you need to know*) (*a waste of time*).

My schoolwork (*is a lot of fun*) (*is very dull and boring*).

This school (*is my idea of a good school*) (*is awful*).

Homework is (*important to do*) (*something I hate*).

Learning out of books is (*fun and I learn a lot*) (*not a good way to learn*).

These responses show consistent points of view, a factor the teacher will want to analyze; they also represent extreme points of view that might be used to measure those responses that fall between the poles. The teacher might use five categories—very positive, somewhat positive, neutral, somewhat negative, very negative—and rate each completed sentence accordingly. After assigning values such as 5-4-3-2-1, he could then compute an average score for each pupil and for the class as a whole. Chapter Nine contains more detailed suggestions for evaluating as well as administering these and other sentence-completion measurements.

## TOOL 3

Date _____

Your number _____

Class _____

### CLUES ABOUT CLASSROOM LIFE

So that members of a class and their teacher may get ideas about how to make life more interesting and important for everybody in the class, each person needs to contribute his or her ideas of what needs to be improved. What things happen that shouldn't happen? What ought to happen but doesn't? Try to imagine you are a detective looking for clues to a "good day" and a "bad day" in your class. Jot down what you might look for or might see to answer these questions. There are no right or wrong answers.

15

---

What are some clues to a good day in our class?  What things happen that are signs of a good day?

1. _____

2. _____

3. _____

4. _____

5. _____

What are some clues to a bad day in our class?  What things happen that are clues that class is not going the way it should or that you would like it to?

1. _____

2. _____

3. _____

4. _____

5. _____

What are some things that should happen a lot more than they do to make it a better class for learning and having fun?

1. _____

2. _____

3. _____

4. _____

5. _____

---

Questions that combine features of both the direct and the indirect approach often may be of great help to the teacher in understanding the classroom atmosphere from the pupils' points of view. Tool 3 illustrates such a third approach: each item directs the pupil's thoughts to a specific aspect of the class, but it allows him to supply his own answers. A teacher can ask young pupils to pretend that they are detectives in search of clues; he can point out to older pupils that in studying their own classroom they are like social scientists, who are detectives of human behavior.

Openness and spontaneity in filling out these forms and during classroom discussions of the results can be increased if the teacher himself answers some of the questions and completes some of the sentences. His responses to items 5, 6, 8, and 9 from Tool 1, his own sentence completions, or his lists of clues and "things that should happen a lot more" from Tool 3 can be presented to the pupils after their forms have been completed and tallied. This can stimulate discussion of the similarities and differences between the teacher's responses and those of the class— as well as of the reasons for them that may help to alter or clarify pupil perceptions of the teacher's attitudes and intentions.

## Measuring Specific Learning Experiences

Sometimes teachers wish to diagnose their pupils' reactions to specific learning experiences, as distinct from the general learning atmosphere. Forms for obtaining such information might be organized like Tool 4.

A growth of joint responsibility for improving classroom procedures will generally result from pupil participation in studying the results. The teacher can designate one group of pupils to tally the number of persons who selected each alternative and another group to read the open-ended portions of each question for useful information on which changes can be based.

## TOOL 4

Date _____

Your number _____

Class _____

### POSTCLASS REACTIONS

Here are some questions about what happened in class today. Circle the letter in front of the statement that best tells how you feel about what happened. There are no right or wrong answers.

1. How much do you feel you learned today?

    a. Don't think I learned much.

    b. Learned a little bit.

    c. Learned quite a lot.

    d. Learned a lot today.

    Please write why you feel this way. _____

2. How clear was it why we were doing _____
   [refer to some specific activity]?

   a. Very clear to me.

   b. Pretty clear to me.

   c. Not so very clear.

   d. Not clear at all.

   What do you think was the reason we did what we did? _____

3. How often did you feel lost during this class period?

   a. Lost most of the time.

   b. Lost quite a few times.

   c. Lost a couple of times.

   d. Not lost at all.

   What made you feel lost? _____

4. How often did you feel you wanted some extra help during this
   class period today?

   a. Wanted help quite a few times.

   b. Wanted help several times.

   c. Wanted a little help once or twice.

   d. Wanted no help.

   What kind of help did you want? _____

5. How often did you see somebody else needing help during our class
   period today?

   a. Saw somebody needing help a lot.

   b. Saw somebody needing help quite a few times.

   c. Saw somebody needing help a few times.

   d. Saw nobody needing help.

   How could they be helped? _____

6. How do you feel about your participation in the discussion this last period?

    a. Not satisfied at all.

    b. Not very satisfied.

    c. Fairly satisfied.

    d. Very satisfied.

    Why do you feel this way? _____

    _____

7. How do you feel about what the teacher did in this last class period?

    a. Very satisfied.

    b. Pretty well satisfied.

    c. Only a little satisfied.

    d. Not satisfied.

    What makes you feel this way? _____

    _____

## Variations for Lower Elementary Grades

Research has shown that it is valid and worthwhile to use sociometric tools for groups of children as young as kindergarten age. But teachers of very young pupils must use fewer and simpler written words in administering diagnostic tools. One technique that has proved useful for finding out the feelings of these pupils is a scale represented by faces; this can serve where the response to an item is in terms of degree of emotional response, from very positive to very negative. The teacher asks the pupils to put an X under the face, such as one of those below, that shows how he feels.

This variation can be used, for example, throughout Tool 4.

The teacher might ask "How did you feel about the things we did during the last period?" He might be more specific, asking the pupils to show their feelings about the spelling lesson or the reading book. If anonymity is not necessary and general class feeling is all that is needed, the teacher might draw the faces on the blackboard and ask for a show of hands after pointing to each face. Even when preserving anonymity, some teachers tabulate the findings on the blackboard and hold a brief discussion about why some pupils marked the unhappy faces and how the next class period might be better. Other teachers simply tally the responses for their own information and make special efforts to interest the pupils who marked the unhappy faces.

## Case Studies

This booklet contains numerous examples of how some of the diagnostic tools have actually been employed to study problem areas in classroom life. These case studies, composites of the authors' experience, suggest not only the variety of such areas but also the general procedures that teachers have followed and certain specific methods they have used to administer the tools, score the responses, and interpret the resulting data.

### Using Direct Measurements

A fifth-grade teacher used Tool 1, Classroom Life, to secure data on the apathy in his classroom. His pupils seemed to lack motivation: they seldom took the initiative in the learning process or introduced new topics that represented their real interests or concerns. As a result the classroom discussions and the atmosphere as a whole tended to be teacher-dominated.

Definite patterns emerged from the analysis of the responses. The pupils generally agreed that whereas "most of the pupils in the class do what the teacher suggests," nonetheless "if we help each other with our work in this class the teacher doesn't like it at all." Although the teacher did want his pupils to help one another, he had obviously not made his wishes clear and had failed to instruct the pupils properly in ways of cooperation in the classroom. As a result the pupils still harbored feelings from previous classroom experiences about the inappropriateness of working together.

Other results indicated that the teacher's goals were only partially achieved. Most pupils replied that they were working "quite hard" on learning, and that they were working "about the same as most" in comparison with others in the class. The teacher interpreted these data to mean that the pupils, as a group, had a rather high work level as a norm. However, all the pupils chose "hardly ever" or "never" in response to the question, "How often do the pupils in this class help one another with their schoolwork?" Again the pupils' failure to perceive that their teacher wanted them to help one another was seen as a probable factor in their low level of academic involvement and group interaction during discussions.

Most of the pupils answered the item beginning "Life in this class with your regular teacher has . . . " with "all good things," "mostly good things," or "more good things than bad." Five pupils, however, chose "more bad things than good." These same pupils, in response to the item beginning "When I'm in this class, I . . . , " chose "am not very interested, bored quite a lot of the time." The teacher was surprised, since he had considered two of these pupils to be quite interested in classroom activities.

These results led the teacher to take constructive action to clarify the pupils' misperceptions of his goals. He planned to make explicit, in words and in action, his desire that they interact and collaborate. He decided also to work more closely with those five pupils who were undermotivated.

## Using Indirect Measurements

A high school English teacher used role playing to stimulate her students' interest and involvement in the plays they were studying.[1] The role playing seemed to go fairly well, but she wanted to check the validity of her observations by objective measurements, since she remembered that a previous class had disliked role playing.

She administered the questions in Tool 3, Clues About Classroom Life, to see how often students selected role playing as a clue to a good day or a bad day and as a thing that should happen a lot more. Role playing was named as the clue to a good day by 85 percent of the students; 10 percent saw it as the clue to a bad day; 5 percent did not mention it. Of those who enjoyed role playing, 75 percent wanted to see it happen a lot more. These results encouraged her to continue role playing and enabled her to identify and help those students who disliked this kind of classroom activity.

## Using Postclass Reactions

A junior high school English teacher wanted to check her impression that her pupils accepted academic tasks passively, carrying out assignments but failing to become involved. She decided to get a series of postclass reactions to determine which classroom procedures caught their interest and which ones bored them.

---

[1]The use of role playing to improve both academic involvement and social interaction is described in M. Chesler and R. Fox, *Role-Playing Methods in the Classroom* (Chicago: Science Research Associates, 1966).

The teacher used three teaching practices for several successive days each: (1) she lectured and questioned directly; (2) she stimulated pupil interaction by having various students lead discussions; and finally (3) she used extensive role playing and creative writing. After each day she administered Tool 4, Postclass Reactions, omitting Question 6, to get the pupils' points of view on each method. She wanted also to get the pupils' direct comparisons of the three methods, so at the end of the experimental sequence of teaching practices she asked them to compare the benefits and inadequacies of each. She prepared questions on how much was learned, the clarity of the lessons, feelings of being lost during the lessons, and feelings of needing extra help. For each question she asked the pupils to tell whether they felt Method 1 was better than 2, whether Method 2 was better than 3, and whether Method 1 was better than 3.

Her own observations during the experiment were confirmed by the daily and the final questionnaires. Methods 2 and 3, rather indirect approaches to teaching, were most effective during the early study of a topic: they stimulated pupil interest and involvement. Method 1, a more direct approach, seemed to work better after the pupils' interest had been aroused and they were willing to listen to the teacher more carefully.

# CHAPTER THREE

# Social Relations in the Classroom

✗ Pupils who feel comfortable with their peers are likely to utilize their academic abilities more fully than those who do not. Research findings show that most pupils who have at least several good friends among their classroom peers will enjoy better mental health and will learn more effectively than pupils who have few or no friends or who are actively disliked.

Furthermore, in a diffuse pattern of classroom friendships, in which almost every member is "most liked" by some other member, pupils tend to have positive feelings toward themselves, perceive the school situation favorably, and make good use of their intellectual potentials. On the other hand, in a narrowly focused pattern of friendships, in which one subgroup of pupils is most popular, another subgroup is most unpopular, and the rest of the pupils have few if any friends, many pupils tend to have negative feelings toward themselves, perceive school unfavorably, and make poor use of their potentials. If, as these findings indicate, successful human relations facilitate a pupil's academic achievement as well as his personal adjustment, the teacher should do everything possible to enhance the emotional support a pupil receives from his peers.

## Measuring Social Relations in the Classroom

When a teacher is considering the social relations in his classroom, he might ask:

23

- Which pupils are not liked by their peers? Why does this seem to be the case?
- Which pupils hold the most influence in the group? How do they come to have the power?
- Which pupils are perceived by their peers as competent students? On what are these judgments based?

Tool 5 is useful for gathering data relevant to classroom liking patterns. Beforehand the teacher should duplicate an alphabetical list of the

## TOOL 5

Date _____

Your number _____

Class _____

### HOW I FEEL ABOUT OTHERS IN MY CLASS

Everybody has different feelings about everybody else. We like some people a lot, some a little bit, and some not at all. Sometimes we think it is not proper or polite to dislike other people, but when we are really honest about it we know that everyone has some negative feelings about some of the people he knows. There are some people you like a lot and some you don't like. There are some people who like you a lot and some who don't like you at all. If the teacher knows the way you really feel about other members of your class, he can often plan things better. There are no right or wrong answers.

1. Which three persons in this class do you personally like the most? Using your class list with names and numbers, write the three numbers in the blanks.

                                                    Pupil's number

   The three I like most are:                       _____

                                                    _____

                                                    _____

2. Which three persons do you personally like the least? Write the numbers in the blanks.

                                                    Pupil's number

   The three I like least are:                      _____

                                                    _____

                                                    _____

3. How many people in this class would you say you know <u>pretty well</u>?

    _____ All of them

    _____ All but a few

    _____ More than half

    _____ About half

    _____ Less than half

    _____ Only a few

4. How many people in this class would you say you like <u>quite a lot</u>?

    _____ All but a few

    _____ More than half

    _____ About half

    _____ Less than half

    _____ Only a few

    _____ None

5. Are there other persons your own age, or younger than you, or older than you, who are not in this class, but whom you like just as much as or more than you like anybody in this class? Yes____ No____

If you answered, yes, please fill in the right spaces below.

<u>Same age as I</u>

Name _____

Name _____

Name _____

<u>Older than I</u>

Name _____ How old? _____

Name _____ How old? _____

Name _____ How old? _____

<u>Younger than I</u>

Name _____ How old? _____

Name _____ How old? _____

Name _____ How old? _____

class members with a number in front of each name; these numbers should not be those assigned to pupils for identification of the forms. Each pupil should receive a copy so that he can refer to it and record his classmates' numbers rather than their names.

Students may require the teacher's support in one special area. Research indicates that everyone forms positive and negative feelings about his associates. These feelings must be recognized as a natural fact of human relations. Negative feelings may be harder for students to accept than positive feelings, for society often frowns on their expression, and most children have been rebuked, at least on a few occasions, for too free an expression of their dislike of someone. At the same time, the expression of negative or critical feelings often is necessary for constructive change and development. Those pupils who fear to express their negative feelings about others even when they might be helpful, or who have not even permitted themselves to accept the fact that they have such feelings, may need reassurance about the naturalness of these feelings. Some help may be needed, too, in the expression of positive feelings. For example, the student who is shy or withdrawn may find it difficult to name anyone whom he likes, or a boy who is attracted to a girl may hesitate to admit it for fear of being razzed by his male peers. At times a pupil may find it hard to express either positive or negative feelings. Treating the task in an objective, routine manner is a real help to pupils who have difficulty in recognizing and expressing the way they feel. The teacher might read the top paragraph of the questionnaire to the class and make sure that everyone understands the confidential nature of the responses.

In addition to liking or disliking certain of their classmates, children attribute to each of them a level of social power, or ability to influence others, and they assess the competence, cooperativeness, and helpfulness of each of their classmates. Tool 6 suggests an approach that can be used to examine these attitudes.

At times a teacher may want to relate the questions to some specific action. For example, if he would like data to use in organizing work teams or planning seating arrangements, he might ask such direct questions as "Which three persons in this class would you most like to sit next to in school?" Such questions should not be asked, however, unless the action is actually planned.

Pupils make judgments about their fellows early in a school year and often maintain these judgments, particularly if no attempts are made to change them. The teacher who wishes to make constructive changes in the classroom atmosphere should reevaluate the nature of the relationships in his classroom throughout the year in order to determine the effectiveness of his efforts.

## Variations for Lower Elementary Grades

Schoolchildren often have formulated certain feelings toward, and evaluations of, their peers at a very young age. Educational modification is often needed to influence these feelings in a positive direction to improve

## TOOL 6

---

Date _____

Your number _____

Class _____

### THE PEOPLE IN MY CLASS

It is a job of teachers to find ways to make school life more interesting and worthwhile for all the students in the class. This form is your chance to give the teacher confidential information that will help him to help each pupil. There are no right or wrong answers. The way you see things is what counts.

1. Which three persons in this class are most often able to get other pupils to do things? Using your class list, write the numbers of the pupils you select.

                                                         Pupil's number

   The three who are most often                          _____

   able to get others to do                              _____

   things are:                                           _____

2. Which three persons in the class do the girls most often do things for?

                                                         Pupil's number

   They are:                                             _____

                                                         _____

                                                         _____

3. Which three persons in the class do the boys most often do things for?

                                                         Pupil's number

   They are:                                             _____

                                                         _____

                                                         _____

4.  Which three persons in this class are most cooperative with the teacher and like to do what the teacher wants the class to do?

Pupil's number

The three most cooperative pupils are:

_____

_____

_____

5.  Which three persons in this class most often go against the teacher and what he would like the class to do?

Pupil's number

The three pupils who most often go against

_____

the teacher are:

_____

_____

6.  Which three persons in this class do you think could make the biggest improvement in their schoolwork if they wanted to?

Pupil's number

The three who could improve most are:

_____

_____

_____

7.  Which three persons in this class do you think show the most ability to learn new things that are taught in school?

Pupil's number

The three best learners are:

_____

_____

_____

8.  Who would you most like to be if you couldn't be yourself but had to be somebody else in this class?

Pupil's number

Who would you most like to be?

_____

Who else would you like to be?

_____

Who else would you like to be?

_____

the mental health of certain pupils and to increase the effectiveness of teaching procedures. As the preceding chapter indicated, modifications in the tools are usually necessary at early grade levels. To measure patterns of classroom liking, one teacher of very young children used a technique similar to the drawings in Chapter Two. She utilized small school photos of each pupil and five plastic freezer boxes with simple faces drawn on them illustrating five degrees of feeling:

| Very nice | Nice | So-so | Not so nice | Not nice at all |

Each child, working privately, sorted the photos and put them into the appropriate boxes according to the way he felt about each person. He was questioned about the reasons for his feelings toward those of his classmates whose pictures he put in the extreme boxes. The teacher who used this method reported that selected sixth-graders had been taught to do an effective and confidential job of testing the younger children individually and recording their responses. The sixth-graders also analyzed the data by constructing matrices and targets of the type described below.

## Analyzing the Data

After the data are collected, they can be tabulated in various ways depending on the problems one is trying to solve. A basic kind of tabulation that gives, perhaps, the greatest amount of information for the least effort is a matrix with as many rows and columns as there are pupils in the class. As shown in the sample below, prepared for a class of sixteen pupils on the liking dimension, positive choices are indicated by 1 and negative choices, or rejections, by $-1$. The order in which each pupil listed his choices is not considered. Each row across contains the choices made by the pupil whose number appears at the left; the columns contain the positive or negative choices received by the pupil whose number appears at the top of the column. By adding the total number of positive and negative entries in each column, the choice pattern is evident at a glance.

29

| | 1 | 2 | 3 | 4 | 5 | 6 | 7 | 8 | 9 | 10 | 11 | 12 | 13 | 14 | 15 | 16 |
|---|---|---|---|---|---|---|---|---|---|---|---|---|---|---|---|---|
| 1 | | 1 | | | 1 | | −1 | | | | 1 | | | −1 | | −1 |
| 2 | 1 | | | | 1 | | −1 | | 1 | | | | −1 | | | −1 |
| 3 | 1 | | | | 1 | | | −1 | | | 1 | | −1 | | −1 | |
| 4 | | 1 | | | 1 | | −1 | | 1 | | | | | −1 | | −1 |
| 5 | 1 | | | 1 | | | | −1 | | | 1 | | | −1 | | −1 |
| 6 | | 1 | 1 | | | | −1 | | | | 1 | | | −1 | | −1 |
| 7 | | 1 | | | | | | | 1 | | 1 | | | −1 | −1 | −1 |
| 8 | | | | 1 | | | 1 | | 1 | | | | −1 | −1 | | −1 |
| 9 | | 1 | | 1 | | | −1 | | | | 1 | | −1 | | −1 | |
| 10 | | 1 | | | 1 | | −1 | | | | 1 | | −1 | −1 | | |
| 11 | | 1 | | | 1 | | | −1 | 1 | | | | −1 | | −1 | |
| 12 | 1 | | | | | | | −1 | 1 | | 1 | | −1 | | | −1 |
| 13 | | | −1 | 1 | 1 | | | | | | 1 | | | −1 | | −1 |
| 14 | | | −1 | 1 | | | | −1 | | | 1 | | −1 | | | 1 |
| 15 | 1 | | −1 | 1 | | | | | −1 | | 1 | | −1 | | | |
| 16 | | | −1 | | −1 | | | | 1 | | 1 | | −1 | | 1 | |
| Total + | 5 | 7 | 0 | 5 | 9 | 0 | 1 | 0 | 7 | 0 | 12 | 0 | 0 | 0 | 1 | 1 |
| Total − | 0 | 0 | 2 | 2 | 1 | 0 | 6 | 5 | 1 | 0 | 0 | 0 | 10 | 8 | 4 | 9 |

## Fig. 1

MATRIX FOR SOCIOMETRIC ANALYSIS

Inspection of this matrix shows a classroom that is rather narrowly focused, with a few very popular pupils, several who are quite unpopular, and others who have few if any friends. Pupil 11 is clearly the star of the class, with twelve positive and no negative choices. Pupils 2, 5, and 9 are also highly liked, although one pupil dislikes 5 and another dislikes 9.

On the negative side, Pupils 13 and 14 are widely disliked, with ten and eight negative choices respectively and no positive choices. They might be thought of as the scapegoats of the class. Pupil 16 is also widely disliked, with nine negative choices and only one positive choice. Pupils 6, 10, and 12 may be thought of as isolates, for they are mentioned by no one, either positively or negatively.

In many cases the choices are mutual. For example, Pupil 1 chose Pupils 2 and 5, and Pupils 2 and 5 similarly chose Pupil 1. Numerous mutual negative choices are also apparent, as between 3 and 13, 4 and 14, and 9 and 15. In these cases the pupils have made their feelings toward each other clear enough to be recognized and reciprocated. But in some cases opposite feelings are expressed. For example, Pupil 7 names 2 as liked, whereas 2 names 7 as not liked. Findings such as these challenge the teacher to try to change perceptions and feelings.

A separate matrix of this kind might be prepared for each dimension —such as liking, influence, or cooperation—that the teacher wants.

To summarize the data from a matrix and point them up more graphically, the target method is useful. To construct a target, draw four concentric circles as shown below.

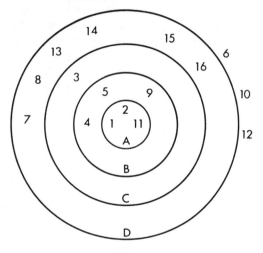

**Fig. 2**

SOCIOMETRIC TARGET

In the center circle, A, the bull's-eye, place the numbers of the pupils who receive more positive choices than would occur if the choices were evenly distributed among all the pupils. If each pupil is asked to choose three others he likes, an even distribution would give each pupil three votes. In this case pupils who receive four or more positive choices and no negative choices are placed in the bull's-eye.

In ring D place the numbers of those pupils who receive four or more negative choices or rejections and one or no positive choices. In ring B place the numbers of those who are more liked than disliked, even though they are not highly chosen. In ring C place the numbers of those who are more disliked than liked. Place the numbers of the neglected pupils outside the whole target. In Fig. 2 the data shown on the matrix (Fig. 1) have been recorded on the target. Different colors might be used for girls and for boys in order to show at a glance whether one sex has higher sociometric status.

Another organization of sociometric data is a series of class maps, or sociograms. A simple procedure is to arrange the class in circular fashion on a large sheet of paper, each pupil being represented by a small circle containing his number. Then lines are drawn between circles to represent choices, a solid line indicating a positive choice, a broken line a negative choice. An arrowhead points toward the person chosen; where there is a mutual choice, there is an arrowhead at each end of the line. Lines of different colors can be used to include more information or to clarify a sociogram.

The sociogram shown in Fig. 3 represents a class of fifteen pupils who were asked to name the person or persons they would most like to sit next to in school and the person or persons they would least like to sit next to. In this case there was no attempt to make them give a specified number of choices. Numbers 1 through 8 in the diagram represent girls; 9 through 15 represent boys.

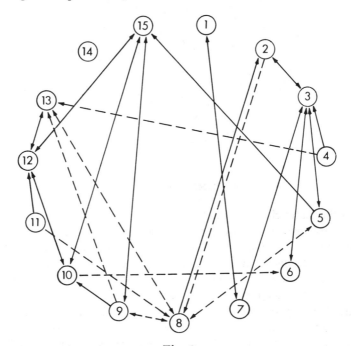

**Fig. 3**

SIMPLE SOCIOGRAM

In this class there is a rather clear split between boys and girls, with only one girl, 5, who makes a positive choice of a boy, 15, and no boys who make positive choices of girls. Among the girls, 3 is the most popular, with five positive choices, three of which are mutual. Moreover, this girl has no negative choices. According to the questionnaires on which the sociogram was based, there are no pupils who would dislike sitting next to her and none whom she rejects. In sharp contrast to this is 8, who is rejected by three boys and two girls. She herself rejects three of these pupils, and the one pupil whom she does choose positively, 2, rejects her. This appears to be a girl who is in trouble from the standpoint of her interpersonal relations, and who needs help. Another person who might be in need of help is 14, who made no choices himself and was chosen by no one. Pupils 4 and 11 were also unchosen by any of their peers. The pattern of choices for Pupil 13 suggests that he has one good friend, 12, but that he is otherwise rather disliked.

To show the structure more clearly, the teacher refined this initial diagram so that the mutual positive choices were close together, as shown in Fig. 4.

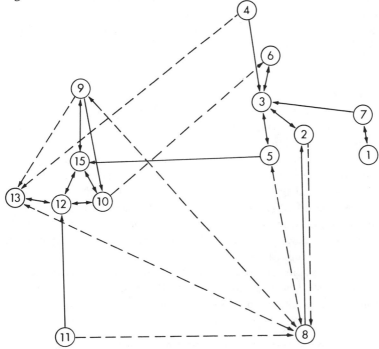

**Fig. 4**

SOCIOGRAM SHOWING SOCIAL DISTANCE

In Fig. 4 the degree of social distance is approximated by the length of the lines. To prepare this type of sociogram, start with the most highly chosen people and then enter the clusters of mutual choices. Some juggling may be necessary to get a clear picture and minimize the crossing of lines. In this sociogram the boy-girl split shows up clearly, particularly in regard to positive choices. The nature of the relations discussed in the preceding paragraph become even clearer, and the cliques and isolates stand out boldly.

A sociogram such as that shown in Fig. 4 contains no more information than the simple sociogram of Fig. 3, but, when the factor of social distance is included, the class structure is apparent at a glance. A sociogram of this type is particularly useful in narrowly focused groups, for stars and scapegoats stand out conspicuously. In diffusely structured classrooms —which are more desirable from the standpoint of mental health—there would be little difference between a simple sociogram and one showing social distance.[1]

Instead of preparing a matrix, a target, or a sociogram, a teacher might find it easier merely to make tallies on the alphabetical name list of his class, recording after each name the number of positive and negative choices a person receives on each of the dimensions being studied. This would not, of course, illustrate how and to whom individual pupils interrelate.

### Using the Data

Data obtained through the tools presented above and analyzed on a matrix, in a sociogram, or in some other way are useful in answering a number of questions.

Which pupils need special help in improving their interpersonal relations because they are rejected or ignored by their peers? By looking at the sociogram or data sheet, the teacher can spot those pupils with a high number of negative choices and those with no choices. These are the pupils who may need special assistance, either from the teacher himself or from some other source. The last section of this chapter contains several action suggestions.

Which pupils are overchosen and which are underchosen? Since pupils are asked on these tools to make three positive and three negative choices, each pupil would receive from two to four choices of both kinds if the choices were nearly evenly distributed. How many pupils receive

---

[1] For more detailed information on the construction of sociograms, see M. Jahoda, M. Deutsch, and S. Cook, *Research Methods in Social Relations,* Part II: "Selected Techniques" (New York: Dryden Press, 1951), pp. 563–69; and H. H. Jennings, *Leadership and Isolation* (New York: Longmans, Green, 1943), pp. 104–11.

one or no choices? How many receive a large number of choices? The target method described is useful for such an analysis.

Which high-influence boys and girls are also liked by their peers? Working from the matrix or from a tabulation, the teacher can list the boys' names, in order of the most liked to the least liked, and make a similar list for girls. A second list can show the most influential boys and girls. The two lists can then be compared to see which pupils of each sex are near the top of both lists. These, clearly, are the leaders in the eyes of the class.

Going further in this direction, are these influential, well-liked pupils seen as good students and cooperative with the teacher, or are some of the most influential pupils in the class seen as being against schoolwork? The comparison of a list showing ratings for cooperation with the lists already made will give this information.

How might pupils be grouped so that certain ones can have a good influence on their peers? The "whom I want to be like" questions may show which good pupils might be the most constructive models for some of the poorer and less motivated pupils.

### A Case Study in Analysis

A sixth-grade teacher at a school in a middle-class neighborhood became concerned over the apathy of her pupils. She felt they needed a greater involvement in their studies and more interest in school; she also felt that they should have more responsibility in making the rules of the classroom. Before starting on any new program, however, she felt that she needed more understanding of the classroom atmosphere.

The teacher decided to use some sociometric questions. She administered the questions about liking in Tool 5, How I Feel About Others in My Class, and those on influence and cooperation in Tool 6, The People in My Class. The administration took about thirty minutes. Later she tabulated the data as shown in Table 1. She put the pupils' numbers down the left side of the page and the sociometric categories across the top. She left extra space between columns so that she might add further analyses. In each column she put the number of choices received by each pupil.

The results offered some meaningful insights into the classroom apathy. In the first place, the data from the liking and influence questions indicated that there was a small, highly liked, and influential elite (Pupils 6, 7, 9, 13, 15, 16, and 19) among both boys and girls. At the same time, a small group of boys (2, 5, 8, and 10) and one girl (14) appeared to be scapegoats for the others. Many of the pupils, especially 17, 18, and 20, were largely neglected by the others, and consequently were hardly involved in classroom or school matters, although they were seen as being rather cooperative with the teacher.

## Table 1

SUMMARY OF SOCIOMETRIC CHOICES

|  | Pupils | Like most | Like least | Influ. girls | Influ. boys | Influ. gen. | Coop. | Uncoop. |
|---|---|---|---|---|---|---|---|---|
|  | 1 | 3 | 2 | 1 | 1 | 2 | 2 | 4 |
|  | 2 | 0 | 15 | 0 | 0 | 0 | 3 | 1 |
| B | 3 | 5 | 2 | 1 | 2 | 3 | 2 | 7 |
| O | 4 | 1 | 7 | 0 | 1 | 1 | 3 | 2 |
| Y | 5 | 0 | 13 | 0 | 0 | 0 | 3 | 1 |
| S | 6 | 6 | 1 | 1 | 4 | 5 | 1 | 7 |
|  | 7 | 7 | 1 | 0 | 4 | 4 | 2 | 6 |
|  | 8 | 0 | 10 | 1 | 1 | 2 | 1 | 2 |
|  | 9 | 8 | 0 | 1 | 6 | 7 | 1 | 4 |
|  | 10 | 0 | 9 | 0 | 0 | 0 | 2 | 1 |
|  | 11 | 3 | 1 | 1 | 0 | 1 | 5 | 1 |
|  | 12 | 3 | 0 | 1 | 0 | 1 | 4 | 2 |
| G | 13 | 12 | 0 | 3 | 2 | 5 | 3 | 6 |
| I | 14 | 0 | 7 | 0 | 0 | 0 | 4 | 1 |
| R | 15 | 13 | 1 | 6 | 2 | 8 | 2 | 4 |
| L | 16 | 10 | 0 | 7 | 1 | 8 | 2 | 3 |
| S | 17 | 0 | 4 | 2 | 0 | 2 | 5 | 0 |
|  | 18 | 0 | 3 | 1 | 0 | 1 | 6 | 2 |
|  | 19 | 9 | 0 | 6 | 1 | 7 | 4 | 3 |
|  | 20 | 0 | 4 | 1 | 1 | 2 | 5 | 3 |

Further, she found that those pupils who were influential tended to be seen as uncooperative with the teacher. Boys 6 and 7 were among the most influential and the least cooperative; among the girls, 13, 15, and 16 were both influential and rather uncooperative.

These findings gave the teacher crucial information about her class. She now had a diagnosis that would provide a basis for action.

### Some Action Suggestions

Detailed consideration of remedial action is beyond the scope of this booklet, but a few suggestions might be made.[2] The teacher can approach remedial action in at least five ways.

First, he can try to help his pupils to perceive as acceptable an expanded variety of individual differences. An effective approach to this end is to develop an inventory of the resources of class members, showing that everyone in the class has some skill or knowledge to offer in different situations. Then, by getting all class members, as a whole or in subgroups, into cooperative activities in which these resources and assets can be used, group standards of what is desirable or of value can often be changed and broadened.

---

[2] Many other action suggestions are elaborated in *Problem Solving to Improve Classroom Learning.*

Second, he can do much to change the patterns of interpersonal relations through different kinds of grouping and work assignments designed to allow the neglected or rejected pupil more participation in planning and carrying out classroom activities. This step can be helpful in changing the way such a child is perceived by his peers and, as a result, raise his skill level.

Third, the teacher can select as "peer helpers" good students who are seen as influential and cooperative with the teacher and whom other pupils want to be like. A forthright arrangement with such a high-status pupil to give support to a child who is experiencing difficulties will often be productive. Peer helpers may be able to reach pupils who need help but who are hard for a teacher to help directly. They can be set up as a panel of specialists in different areas who are ready to help any pupil on request, or they can be paired with other pupils on such specific tasks as spelling drill, correcting arithmetic papers, or working on special projects and preparing a report. One must be careful, however, not to force peer help on a pupil who is unwilling to accept it. It should also be kept in mind that the helper, no matter how capable, is likely to need some assistance from the teacher in developing the strategy or the skills necessary to be an effective assistant.

Fourth, the teacher can work on getting subgroups to relate productively and positively to each other in the classroom. When subgroups are so antagonistic that there is a schism in the class, the teacher is challenged to reduce this schism and unify the group. Often it is possible to change the relationship between two antagonistic subgroups into wholesome competition, which leads to increased interpersonal understanding and psychological maturity.

Fifth, he can work directly with rejected or neglected individuals. Frank, friendly discussions with the pupil or his parents, in which the pupil knows that his confidence will be respected, can often be very helpful. In such discussions the teacher can often use the reasons other pupils gave for rejecting him. The teacher may be able to help him correct certain characteristics or behavior that contribute to this lack of acceptance by his peers.

Role playing offers many possibilities for constructive action on both the individual and the group level. It is particularly useful in improving a person's understanding of the feelings of others and in improving social skills.[3]

In working with a disliked child who seems unable to develop a posi-

---

[3] Much helpful material on role playing—when and how to use it in the classroom, together with many suggested role-playing activities—will be found in *Role-Playing Methods in the Classroom.*

tive relationship with his peers, the teacher's first aim might be to help him develop positive relations with the teacher and then expand these to include members of his peer group. A combination of individual work with a pupil outside class and work in the class with the help of class leaders is often an effective approach. For the child whose isolation or rejection is the result of shyness and lack of social initiative, poor personal hygiene, or some similar condition, the problem can usually be handled by the teacher. On the other hand, the isolated or rejected child may have serious problems beyond the scope of remedial action on the part of the teacher alone. In such cases the teacher will want to utilize whatever school personnel services are available and appropriate, such as a visiting teacher, counselor, or school psychologist. In some cases referral to a child-guidance clinic may be desirable.

As social relationships in a classroom are improved, academic achievement can be expected to increase and the job of the teacher will be accomplished more effectively.

# CHAPTER FOUR

# Pupil Norms
# in Classroom Life

Norms, standards, or expectations exist in all social groups to cover virtually all aspects of human behavior. Subgroups or individuals often establish expectations of behavior that are different from those of the larger group. Among the most familiar and controversial norms are those of teen-agers, who are often more anxious to conform to the expectations of their peers than to those of the influential adults in their lives.

In the classroom it is important for the teacher to know that in addition to the expectations or standards he may have for the performance or behavior of the pupils, the classroom peer group may have some standards of its own. These peer-group norms may be supportive of the teacher's expectations or they may be at cross purposes with them.

But norms are not easily apparent. Seldom is there complete unanimity in a group as to what is "the thing to do." Each pupil has his own private ideas about the proper thing to do in a given circumstance; he probably knows what the teacher expects; and he has some notion about what some of the other pupils expect. His actual behavior will be the result of the extent to which he allows each of these various expectations to influence him.

Can the teacher discover the group's norms for classroom behavior by asking each pupil what he thinks are the standards held by the majority of the class, or is the group norm the sum of the expectations held by each individual child for himself? How can a teacher discover which are standards actually subscribed to by the peer group and which are merely reflections of his own standards for the class, parroted back to him in an attempt to please?

For the purpose of our discussion, peer-group norms are considered a composite of the perceptions held by the class members regarding what the other pupils feel is appropriate to do. It's what the pupil *thinks* is the group norm that will influence his behavior.

The teacher may discover that pupils are misperceiving the attitudes of their classmates and are attributing to them standards they don't really hold. Nevertheless, the group standard that has effect at the moment is that which is thought by most of the pupils to be what the others in the class accept. A summary of individually held pupil standards becomes a group standard only when the pupils *perceive* it to be the group standard.

### Problems in Measuring Norms

A teacher can begin his inquiry into the norms of his classroom by asking himself such questions as the following:

- Is it "the thing to do" in my classroom to cooperate with the teacher, or does group approval go to the pupil who attempts to obstruct, divert, or embarrass me?
- Do the pupils think that I'm for them, or against them?
- Do they feel that it's all right for one pupil to ask another for help in this classroom? that it's a good idea to work hard on schoolwork, or that it's best to do just enough to get by?

He may quickly find out that there is not agreement by all pupils regarding these matters. For example, five underachieving boys in a sixth-grade classroom may agree that schoolwork is not worth the effort; that the teacher is not to be respected for his knowledge or teaching skill, but to be feared for his authority; that good school achievement is "sissy"; and that physical aggressiveness is the best way to gain the admiration of one's peers. These attitudes may remain within this small clique; they may, however, be widely held by others in the classroom if these boys are highly influential in the social structure.

A teacher might find that although Tool 1 reveals nearly all pupils to be interested in academic activities, classroom involvement and interaction is minimal. Each pupil may assert that he himself likes school and feels the teacher is giving reasonable assignments, but also state that most kids in this class think schoolwork is too hard and that school is no fun. Here is confusion between the individual attitudes and what is perceived as being the group norm, to which one must attempt to conform. Such a perceived group norm, however inaccurate, can be quite potent in influencing pupil behavior.

These examples show that the teacher must probe deeply for meaningful data and must ask questions other than "Is this or that the standard?"

The following questions will help show the complexity of measuring classroom norms:

- How accurate are individual pupils in perceiving group norms and to what extent do individual pupil attitudes agree with the perceived group norms?
- Is the teacher himself accurate in perceiving the norms of his classroom?
- Do pupils think the teacher supports the pupil-held norms or differs from them in his thinking?

## Measuring the Classroom Norms

Evaluation can begin with the construction of a tool, such as Tool 7, that lists a series of possible norms in the form of propositions, and asks the individual pupils to indicate how many pupils in the class agree with each proposition. A teacher might use the statements in Tool 7 or construct others more pertinent to particular conditions in his classroom.

Tool 7 will reveal what individual pupils perceive the group norms to be. By making a few modifications in it, as shown in Tool 8, the teacher can determine the attitudes held by the individual pupils themselves.

The pupil's perceptions of how well the teacher agrees with the standards of the peer group can be ascertained by some further modifications in the headings and directions of Tool 7, as shown in Tool 9.

To compare his own ideas with those of the class, the teacher can complete Tool 8 before looking at data from the pupils' forms.

### Understanding the Data

The meaningfulness as well as the complexity of the data can be seen by studying the congruences and discrepancies between the separate measurements, including the teacher's responses to Tool 8.

- *Perceived classroom norms:* a tabulation of the results of Tool 7.

Methods of tabulating the responses and arriving at the median, or "average," results are described as a part of the case study in the next section of this chapter.

- *Congruence of perceived norms and individual standards:* the discrepancy between what the pupils perceived as the classroom norms, measured by Tool 7, and the individual standards seen collectively, tabulated from Tool 8.

41

## TOOL 7

Date _____

Your number _____

Class _____

### HOW THIS CLASS FEELS

School classes are quite different from one another in how pupils
think and feel about schoolwork, about one another, and about teachers.
How do you think your classmates feel about the following things? Put
a check in one of the boxes under "How Many Feel This Way?" for each
of the statements below. There are no right or wrong answers.

How Many Feel This Way?

| | Almost all | Many | About half | Some | Only a few |
|---|---|---|---|---|---|
| 1. It is good to take part as much as possible in classroom work. | | | | | |
| 2. Asking the teacher for help is a good thing to do. | | | | | |
| 3. It is good to help other pupils with their schoolwork except during tests. | | | | | |
| 4. Schoolwork is more often fun than it is not fun. | | | | | |
| 5. Our teacher really understands how pupils feel. | | | | | |

If the individually held standards are different from those perceived as
being group norms, there is probably little communication between pupils,
and what is perceived as the norm is not the real norm. Action is needed
to stimulate greater awareness on the part of individuals and the class
as a whole.

- *Congruence of the individual pupil's perception of the norms
  and the actual consensus:* the discrepancy between a pupil's responses to Tool 7 and the responses of the rest of the class to it.

## TOOL 8

Date_____

Your number_____

Class_____

HOW DO YOU FEEL ABOUT THESE THINGS?

Put a check in the box that tells how you feel about each of the statements below. There are no right or wrong answers.

|  | I agree almost always | I agree more than I disagree | I agree as often as I disagree | I disagree more than I agree | I disagree almost always |
|---|---|---|---|---|---|
| 1. It is good to take part as much as possible in classroom work. |  |  |  |  |  |
| 2. Asking the teacher for help is a good thing to do. |  |  |  |  |  |

If a pupil's perception of the norm is inaccurate, he may be either insensitive to the norm or actually isolated from the group.

- *Congruence of a pupil's own standards and what he perceives as the classroom norms:* the discrepancy between a pupil's responses on Tool 7 and on Tool 8.

If a pupil's personal opinions are quite different from his judgments of the classroom norms, he may consciously feel alienated or different from his classmates, a condition that may require remedial action.

- *Congruence of the teacher's norms and the pupils' perceptions of the classroom norms:* comparison of the results of Tool 7 and the teacher's responses to Tool 8.

If the teacher's opinions of what is desirable in the classroom are quite different from that of the majority of the class, action is needed to improve pupil-teacher communication and mutual understanding.

- *Congruence of the pupils' perceptions of class norms and their perceptions of the teacher's opinions:* comparison of the tabulated results of Tool 7 and Tool 9.

Where such a comparison reveals a substantial discrepancy, there is possible alienation or poor communication—or both—and a probable need for further study and remedial action.

- *Congruence of the teacher's actual opinion and the pupils' perceptions of it:* comparison of responses to Tool 9 and the teacher's responses to Tool 8.

If there is much discrepancy, more effective pupil-teacher communication is needed here also.

## TOOL 9

Date_____

Your number_____

Class_____

HOW DO YOU THINK YOUR TEACHER FEELS?

Put a check in the box that tells how you think your teacher feels about each of the statements below.  There are no right or wrong answers.

| | He would agree almost always | He would agree more than disagree | He would agree as often as disagree | He would disagree more than agree | He would disagree almost always |
|---|---|---|---|---|---|
| 1. It is good to take part as much as possible in classroom work. | | | | | |
| 2. Asking the teacher for help is a good thing to do. | | | | | |

## A Case Study

A fifth-grade teacher wanted her class to utilize these tools on classroom norms, so she explained her purpose to them as follows:

"I'd be interested in finding out how people in this class think about some of the things we do together in this classroom. We could just talk about your ideas, but perhaps it would help you to think about your ideas first and record them on paper. Then we can discuss them later. I've prepared some materials that will make it easy for you."

The administration took about thirty minutes. While the pupils were filling out their forms, the teacher completed Tool 8, recording her own perceptions.

### Tabulation and Analysis

Using a blank copy of Tool 7, the teacher tabulated the data from the pupils by recording the frequency with which each response was checked. She used what is technically called the median, or middle, frequency: twenty-one pupils responded, so the eleventh pupil, counting from either end of the distribution, was the middle, or median, pupil. She drew a box around the category into which this median pupil fell; this category represented the class norm. Her data are shown in Table 2.

### Table 2

HOW THIS CLASS FEELS

| | Almost all | Many | About half | Some | Only a few |
|---|---|---|---|---|---|
| 1. It is good to take part as much as possible in classroom work. | 2 | 15 | 4 | 0 | 0 |
| 2. Asking the teacher for help is a good thing to do. | 7 | 9 | 1 | 4 | 0 |
| 3. It is good to help other pupils with their schoolwork except during tests. | 4 | 5 | 6 | 2 | 4 |
| 4. Schoolwork is more often fun than it is not fun. | 2 | 5 | 10 | 2 | 2 |
| 5. The teacher really understands how pupils feel. | 8 | 6 | 6 | 1 | 0 |

The teacher then compared each pupil's responses to Tool 7 with the class norm, shown in Table 2, to determine the extent to which he accurately perceived each group norm. The category representing the class norm became the basic point for computing an individual's scores. If his **45** response agreed entirely with the norm category, the teacher entered a 0 in his row under that norm column in Table 3; if he responded one or more categories to the left (a more positive response than the norm), a +1, +2, and so on; if one or more categories to the right (more negative), a −1, −2, and so on. A question mark would have been used had a pupil not recorded a particular response. A large number of zeros in any column indicate wide pupil agreement as to what a norm is; a preponderance of pluses or minuses, wide disagreement. Many zeros in a pupil's row indicate a high degree of accuracy in perceiving the norms; many pluses and minuses, inaccuracy.

## Table 3

### PUPIL ACCURACY IN PREDICTING GROUP NORMS

| | Statement About Life in the Classroom | | | | |
|---|---|---|---|---|---|
| Pupil | Good to take part | Good to ask teacher | Good to help others | Schoolwork more fun | Teacher really understands |
| 1 | −1 | −1 | −1 | 0 | −1 |
| 2 | 0 | −2 | −1 | −2 | −1 |
| 3 | 0 | 0 | +2 | +2 | −1 |
| 4 | 0 | +1 | +2 | −2 | 0 |
| 5 | 0 | +1 | +1 | +1 | 0 |
| 6 | 0 | 0 | 0 | 0 | 0 |
| 7 | 0 | 0 | −2 | 0 | 0 |
| 8 | 0 | +1 | +2 | +1 | 0 |
| 9 | 0 | −2 | +1 | +1 | −1 |
| 10 | 0 | 0 | 0 | 0 | 0 |
| 11 | −1 | 0 | 0 | 0 | 0 |
| 12 | −1 | +1 | 0 | −1 | 0 |
| 13 | 0 | 0 | 0 | 0 | 0 |
| 14 | +1 | +1 | +1 | +1 | 0 |
| 15 | 0 | −2 | −2 | 0 | 0 |
| 16 | −1 | −2 | −2 | −1 | −2 |
| 17 | +1 | +1 | +1 | +1 | 0 |
| 18 | 0 | 0 | −2 | 0 | −1 |
| 19 | 0 | 0 | 0 | 0 | −1 |
| 20 | 0 | +1 | +1 | 0 | 0 |

The teacher made several observations about pupil accuracy from a quick study of Table 3. Pupil 16 was the least accurate in predicting the group norms, failing in all five cases. Pupils 1, 2, 9, 14, 16, and 17 were all quite inaccurate: 1, 2, and 16 were more negative than the actual norm; 14 and 17 were more positive; 9 was balanced on both sides. Pupils 6, 10, and 13 most accurately predicted each of the group standards.

Table 4 shows the congruence of each pupil's standards recorded in Tool 8 with the group norms determined in Table 2. The scoring technique was the same as that used in Table 3. A large number of zeros in a column indicates that the pupils as individuals tended to agree with the group norms; a preponderance of pluses or minuses, that they tended to disagree. Many zeros in a pupil's row indicate a high correlation of his norms with those of the group; many pluses or minuses, a low correlation.

Several observations were possible from this tabulation. Pupil 15 agreed with the group norm in every instance. Other pupils with a high correlation were 1, 10, 11, 13, 14, 18, and 20. No pupil disagreed entirely, but Pupil 9 differed in three of the five cases and by as much as three categories. Other pupils with a low correlation were 2, 7, 8, and 12, also disagreeing in three of the five cases.

As one reads down the columns, it appears that there is excellent agreement between individual standards and the perceived group norm regarding "Asking the teacher for help is a good thing to do" (all 0 but one). On the other hand, quite a number of pupils gave a higher rating to the variable "schoolwork is fun" than they thought would be given by their classmates (nine pupils with +1 scores).

## Table 4

### INDIVIDUAL PUPIL AGREEMENT WITH GROUP NORMS

*Statement About Life in the Classroom*

| Pupil | Good to take part | Good to ask teacher | Good to help others | Schoolwork more fun | Teacher really understands |
|-------|-------------------|---------------------|---------------------|---------------------|----------------------------|
| 1 | 0 | 0 | 0 | 0 | −1 |
| 2 | −1 | 0 | −1 | −2 | 0 |
| 3 | 0 | 0 | 0 | −1 | −3 |
| 4 | +1 | 0 | −2 | 0 | 0 |
| 5 | +1 | 0 | 0 | +0 | 0 |
| 6 | 0 | 0 | −1 | 0 | −1 |
| 7 | +1 | 0 | −2 | +1 | 0 |
| 8 | +1 | 0 | −2 | +1 | 0 |
| 9 | −3 | 0 | −2 | 0 | −1 |
| 10 | 0 | 0 | 0 | +1 | 0 |
| 11 | 0 | 0 | +1 | 0 | 0 |
| 12 | +1 | −1 | 0 | +1 | 0 |
| 13 | +1 | 0 | 0 | 0 | 0 |
| 14 | 0 | 0 | 0 | +1 | 0 |
| 15 | 0 | 0 | 0 | 0 | 0 |
| 16 | 0 | 0 | −2 | 0 | −1 |
| 17 | 0 | 0 | −2 | +1 | 0 |
| 18 | 0 | 0 | 0 | +1 | 0 |
| 19 | +0 | 0 | 0 | +1 | 0 |
| 20 | +1 | 0 | 0 | 0 | 0 |
| 21 | +1 | 0 | 0 | −1 | 0 |

The teacher also organized data from pupil responses to Tool 8 to show frequency of response to each category (Table 5), thus making

possible a direct comparison of the summary of pupils' individual standards with what they thought were the group norms (Table 2). She noted
that the boxes placed around the category containing the median pupil
occurred in positions identical with those in Table 2, although there were
some variations in the actual frequency distribution.

## Table 5

### SUMMARY OF INDIVIDUAL PUPIL'S STANDARDS

| | I agree almost always | I agree more than I disagree | I agree as often as I disagree | I disagree more than I agree | I disagree almost always |
|---|---|---|---|---|---|
| 1. It is good to take part as much as possible in class-room work. | 9 | 10 | 1 | 0 | 1 |
| 2. Asking the teacher for help is a good thing to do. | 0 | 20 | 1 | 0 | 0 |
| 3. It is good to help other pupils with their school-work except during tests. | 0 | 1 | 12 | 2 | 6 |
| 4. Schoolwork is more often fun than it is not fun. | 0 | 9 | 9 | 2 | 1 |
| 5. The teacher really under-stands how pupils feel. | 0 | 16 | 4 | 0 | 1 |

Thus the teacher was reassured that relatively good communication
existed among the pupils regarding the aspects of classroom life measured
by these instruments; that a summary of individually held standards
matched quite closely the norms attributed by the pupils to their classmates.

Table 6, constructed like the preceding two, compares pupil judgments
of the teacher's norms, recorded on Tool 9, with the group norms shown
in Table 2. A large number of zeros in a column indicate that the class
tends to feel that the teacher agrees with its norms; a preponderance of
pluses or minuses, that she disagrees. Many zeros in a pupil's row indicate that he perceives the teacher as agreeing with the group norm;
many pluses or minuses, as disagreeing.

The teacher was able to see the overall class perception of her norms
as well as how each pupil understood her attitudes. She found that the
class tended to view her as somewhat unrealistic about life in the classroom. For example:

- Sixteen of twenty-one pupils believed that she "almost always"
  thought it good to take part in classroom work, whereas the group
  standard in Table 2 was a step below this: that is, "many" pupils
  thought so, but not "almost all."

- Eleven of twenty-one pupils believed that she "almost always" thought that schoolwork was fun, whereas the group standard was two steps below this: only about half the class thought schoolwork was fun.

## Table 6

DEGREE TO WHICH PUPIL THINKS TEACHER AGREES
WITH GROUP NORMS

*Statement About Life in the Classroom*

| Pupil | Good to take part | Good to ask teacher | Good to help others | Schoolwork more fun | Teacher really understands |
|-------|-------------------|---------------------|---------------------|---------------------|----------------------------|
| 1 | 0 | −2 | 0 | 0 | 0 |
| 2 | 0 | −1 | −1 | 0 | −3 |
| 3 | +1 | 0 | +1 | +1 | 0 |
| 4 | 0 | 0 | −2 | +1 | 0 |
| 5 | +1 | 0 | +1 | +1 | 0 |
| 6 | +1 | −1 | −1 | +1 | 0 |
| 7 | +1 | 0 | −2 | 0 | 0 |
| 8 | +1 | 0 | −2 | +1 | 0 |
| 9 | −3 | 0 | 0 | −1 | −1 |
| 10 | 0 | 0 | 0 | −2 | −3 |
| 11 | +1 | 0 | 0 | 0 | 0 |
| 12 | +1 | 0 | 0 | 0 | 0 |
| 13 | +1 | +1 | 0 | 0 | 0 |
| 14 | +1 | 0 | +1 | +1 | 0 |
| 15 | +1 | 0 | 0 | +1 | 0 |
| 16 | +1 | 0 | −2 | 0 | 0 |
| 17 | +1 | 0 | −2 | +1 | 0 |
| 18 | +1 | 0 | 0 | +1 | 0 |
| 19 | +1 | +1 | +1 | +1 | 0 |
| 20 | +1 | 0 | 0 | +1 | 0 |
| 21 | +1 | −1 | +1 | 0 | 0 |

There were other noticeable if less striking deviations. Pupils 2 and 10 registered highly atypical feelings that the teacher would disagree with the proposition that she "really understands how pupils feel." Four pupils (1, 2, 6, and 21) felt the teacher was less positive about pupils asking for help than were the pupils themselves. Seven pupils (2, 4, 6, 7, 8, 16, and 17) thought the teacher felt considerably less positive than did the class about the desirability of helping others with schoolwork, whereas five (3, 5, 14, 19, and 21) saw her as more positive.

## Action Taken

Since most disagreement centered on pupils' helping one another, the teacher reexamined her own thinking and her communication with the pupils. She concluded that she had been overly concerned with individual achievement, with each person doing his own work, primarily as a grading factor. After another class discussion, on "When and how can we help each other?" she found it feasible to give additional opportunities for cooperative classroom learning. Seats were grouped in twos and threes, and rules were developed governing talking in class that permitted sharing between study partners during study periods.

The teacher made a special effort to reach the four pupils who felt she did not like to be asked for help. She used role playing as one device to explore pupils' feelings about asking for help and adults' problems in giving help.

To promote greater communication among pupils on group standards, the teacher set up a steering committee to provide leadership in classroom improvement. This committee observed classroom procedures, discussed implications, and brought recommendations to the class once a week.[1]

Finally, the teacher planned a long-range schedule for administering other tools that could provide additional insights into other aspects of classrooom life, including measurements covering influences on the pupils' lives both inside and outside the classroom.

---

[1] See *Problem Solving to Improve Classroom Learning* for greater detail on how such a committee might be established, how it would operate, and what effect it might have on the class.

# CHAPTER FIVE

# Pupil-Teacher Interaction

A teacher's behavior in his classroom is a continuing process of interaction with his pupils. At times the interaction is so complex and subtle that the teacher may be unaware of certain aspects of it. Thus a discrepancy often exists between a teacher's goals and his actual behavior in the classroom. Similarly, there is likely to be a marked discrepancy between a teacher's perceptions of his behavior in the classroom and his pupils' perceptions of that same behavior. When such a situation exists, the teacher's classroom practices are not contributing effectively to the accomplishment of teaching objectives. A teacher may, for instance, wish to be seen as a warm and friendly person in order to help the pupils feel comfortable, but the pupils may see his behavior as threatening or punitive. In such cases classroom atmosphere and events are influenced more by unconscious factors than by the teacher's conscious philosophy of education.

Many teachers are eager to learn about the discrepancies between their objectives and practices. Data from disinterested observation or tape recordings of a class session provide a view of exactly what happened, but they require that some systematic criteria be used to evaluate the teacher's actual behavior in relation to what he has intended to do to reach his teaching objectives. Pupils' perceptions of the teacher's behavior can provide similar comparisons of goals and practices.

## Measuring Pupil-Teacher Interaction

Because the classroom is a different psychological setting for each of its participants, a complete analysis of the dynamics of classroom activity requires information from all points of view.

### Pupil Points of View

Tool 10 uses items of typical concern in pupil-teacher interaction, but a teacher may wish to revise the questions to reflect his own classroom situation more closely. It might be used in conjunction with other tools, such as 1, 4, or 9, which elicit certain student perceptions of the teacher's behavior. This form has been used effectively as low as the fourth grade and occasionally in the third. In these lower grades the teacher should explain the questions in concrete terms, not only to clarify the meanings of the words, but also to demonstrate exactly what is meant by "talking to the whole class," "talking to individual pupils," and "talking about work or about behavior."

### TOOL 10

Date _____

Your number _____

Class _____

#### PUPIL PERCEPTIONS OF A CLASS PERIOD

Think about the last hour of class. About how much time would you say was spent in each of the following activities? Draw a circle around the answer you think best tells how much time was spent. There are no right or wrong answers.

How much time?     (Circle one)

1. The teacher talking to the whole class--telling, answering, or asking something

   a lot    some    a little    none

2. The teacher talking to individual pupils--telling, answering, or asking something

   a lot    some    a little    none

3. Pupils talking to the teacher-- telling, answering, or asking something

   a lot    some    a little    none

Now think about what you yourself did during the last class hour. Write in the number you think is right. Make the best guess you can.

4. My teacher told or asked me things or answered my questions _____ times.

5. I told or asked my teacher things or answered his questions _____ times.

6. I told or asked other pupils things or answered their questions
_____ times.

7. During the last class hour, my teacher told or asked me things or answered my questions

              a. _____ much more than most other pupils

check    b. _____ a little more than most other pupils

one      c. _____ a little less than most other pupils

              d. _____ much less than most other pupils

8. I volunteered to say things or do things during the class hour

              a. _____ much more than most other pupils

check    b. _____ a little more than most other pupils

one      c. _____ a little less than most other pupils

              d. _____ much less than most other pupils

9. When my teacher told or asked me something, it was

              a. _____ only about my work

check    b. _____ mostly about my work, but a little about my behavior

one      c. _____ mostly about my behavior, but a little about my work

              d. _____ only about my behavior

10. When my teacher told or asked me something, he was

              a. _____ very pleased

check    b. _____ satisfied

one      c. _____ somewhat dissatisfied

              d. _____ quite dissatisfied

Responses from Tool 10 will show whether there are any individual pupils or subgroups of pupils who see themselves as overparticipating or underparticipating. They will also show pupils' perceptions of (1) the relative participation of teacher and pupils, (2) whether the interaction was related to work or to behavior, and (3) the teacher's degree of satisfaction with the individual pupil.

**Objective Observation**

An impartial observer, preferably another teacher who is familiar with similar classroom routine at a similar grade level, can collect data that offer useful clues to areas in which a teacher might increase his teaching effectiveness: aspects of his behavior that are confusing or disruptive; a section of the class that he is ignoring; pupils whom he is treating differently from others. There are several observational methods that can be used to provide the teacher with such feedback on his classroom behavior. Before an observer comes to the classroom, the teacher should explain to the pupils what this visitor will be doing and some of the reasons why he is observing.

One method classifies classroom interaction by its origin and direction: teacher to the whole class; teacher to individual pupils; and pupils to the teacher. Within each classification the action is further categorized as to whether it is oriented to work or to social behavior and social control. Finally, the specific nature of each behavior is identified. The following outline classifies the interactions and defines each type of behavior.

I. Teacher to the whole class
   A. Work
      1. Telling and giving information: transmitting fact, opinion, and the like directly to the whole class about subject matter or related areas of classroom interest
      2. Giving directions: telling the class what to do or how to do a particular piece of work
      3. Asking and indirect probing: trying to get information from the class or posing questions to the whole class regarding classroom work
   B. Social behavior and social control
      1. Positive: indicating to the whole class that its social behavior and control have been good
      2. Neutral: giving directions or information with no evaluation implied
      3. Negative: indicating to the whole class that its social conduct has not been good
II. Teacher to individual pupils
   A. Work
      1. Positive: rewarding comments directed to an individual pupil about an aspect of his work
      2. Neutral: comments or questions that are neither rewarding nor punishing directed to an individual pupil about an aspect of his work
      3. Negative: punishing comments directed to an individual pupil about an aspect of his work

B. Social behavior and social control
1. Positive: rewarding comments directed to an individual pupil about his social conduct in the class
2. Neutral: Comments or questions that are neither rewarding nor punishing directed to an individual pupil about his conduct in the class
3. Negative: punishing comments directed to an individual pupil about his conduct in the class
III. Pupils to teacher
A. Work
1. Contributions: pupil remarks, such as elaboration or helpful comments, that add something to class activities or assignments
2. Dependent and asking questions: pupil remarks that either show dependency on the teacher or are questions about work that is to be done
B. Social behavior and social control
1. Complaints: pupil remarks about conduct of other pupils in the class
2. Attention seeking: pupil remarks aimed at getting attention from the teacher or other pupils, or both

Tool 11 is a suggested format for recording the instances of behavior in each category that occur during the classroom observation period. The entries are data that were collected during one five-minute period of a high school business class while the teacher was introducing the idea of a classroom simulation of a retail store. The observer marked a category for each observed unit of behavior, defined as one complete statement or one uninterrupted sequence of statements that fell within a single category. The symbol 1 represents a unit directed to the whole class; 0, a unit to or from a girl; X, a unit to or from a boy.

These data indicate that, for the most part, the teacher was giving information and directions; reacting in a neutral manner; evoking dependency responses; reacting toward more girls than boys; and receiving behavior from girls and boys equally. The teacher was especially interested in these results, since he had thought that he was rewarding students for good responses rather than behaving neutrally, and that he was evoking many contributions from the pupils rather than the few that occurred.

In the observations of this class, and in such observations generally, a new Tool 11 form should be used for each five-minute sequence. This permits study of changes in patterns of interaction during the class period. After every two five-minute sequences, observers should fill in a form such as Tool 12 to show the activities and methods of participation used during the preceding ten minutes. An observer can generally remember

## TOOL 11

---

CLASSROOM OBSERVATION SCHEDULE

Teacher or Class _____ Date _____ Time _____

### I.   Teacher to Whole Class

A.   Work

B.   Social Behavior and Social Control

| 1.  Giving information | 2.  Giving directions | 3.  Asking; probing | 1.  Positive | 2.  Neutral | 3.  Negative |
|---|---|---|---|---|---|
| ℍℍ III | II | I | | II | I |

### II.   Teacher to Individual Pupils

A.   Work

B.   Social Behavior and Social Control

| 1.  Positive | 2.  Neutral | 3.  Negative | 1.  Positive | 2.  Neutral | 3.  Negative |
|---|---|---|---|---|---|
| 00 | 0000X<br>XX00<br>000 | X0 | | X | XX |

### III.   Pupils to Teacher

A.   Work

B.   Social Behavior and Social Control

| 1.  Contributions | 2.  Dependent | 1.  Complaints | 2.  Attention seeking |
|---|---|---|---|
| 0X0 | 0000XX<br>XXX0X0<br>0 | X | X |

---

what portion of a class was engaged in the various types of activities listed.

The teacher and the observer should work together in tabulating and interpreting the data; they can use various methods, depending on what the teacher wants to know about his classroom behavior.

Perhaps the teacher wants to know what proportion of behaviors are aimed at the whole class and what proportion to individuals; he might want to know how much time he spends giving negative comments related to social control or to work. Perhaps he wants to compare the number of dependency responses with the number of contributions. Perhaps he wants to see how the pupils have perceived what he has done by comparing what the observer has seen with what the pupils have perceived: Do the pupils and the observer see his behavior as positive, see him as being satisfied with the pupils—or do the pupils and the observer see things differently? If there is a discrepancy in perceptions, the teacher might ask why, for example, the pupils sometimes see him as dissatisfied when he is trying to show satisfaction. Another important thing for the teacher to look for is whether he is behaving differently towards girls than boys. Differential relationships with the two sexes often occur quite unconsciously, and research has shown that teachers often indicate more satisfaction with girls than with boys.[1]

## TOOL 12

---

CLASSROOM OBSERVATION SCHEDULE

Teacher or Class _____ Date _____ Time _____

What methods of participation have been used for the last ten minutes? Check all appropriate items.

|  | Whole class | Small groups | Individuals |
|---|---|---|---|
| 1. Lecturing, listening, looking, etc. | _____ | _____ | _____ |
| 2. Practicing, oral drill, trying out | _____ | _____ | _____ |
| 3. Being tested, quizzed | _____ | _____ | _____ |
| 4. Game, contest, competing | _____ | _____ | _____ |
| 5. Discussion | _____ | _____ | _____ |
| 6. Reading, studying | _____ | _____ | _____ |
| 7. Writing | _____ | _____ | _____ |
| 8. Creating and making | _____ | _____ | _____ |

COMMENTS: _____

_____

---

[1]R. Schmuck and E. Van Egmond, "Sex Differences in the Relationship of Interpersonal Perceptions to Academic Performance," *Psychology in the Schools*, 2, No. 1 (January 1965), 32–40.

Perhaps he wants to know which kind of teaching behavior, direct or indirect (as described in the third case study in Chapter Two), is the more effective. He can find out about this by trying to be direct for a week or so, telling and giving information as well as giving directions, and then being indirect for a comparable period, using indirect probing. Then, by means of instruments presented in Chapter Two, he can evaluate how well each of the teaching procedures worked for the pupils.

Many other systems for observing classroom behavior and interaction have been used.[2] One of the most valuable in the hands of a skilled observer is "interaction analysis," developed by Flanders. The central concern of this system is the amount of freedom the teacher grants the student. It assumes that in a given situation a teacher has a choice: "He can be direct, that is, minimizing the freedom of the student to respond. His choice, conscious or unconscious, depends upon many factors, among which are his perceptions of the situation and the goals of the particular learning situation."[3] The system provides also for categorizing student talk and for identifying periods of silence or confusion. Types of oral behavior of teacher and students are subdivided in order to make the total pattern of interaction more meaningful. All together, there are ten categories, described in Tool 13, which cover all oral interaction occurring in a classroom.[4]

Flanders remarks that interaction analysis—

"consists simply of observing, recording, and counting events as they occur. The usefulness of such a simple procedure will depend on congruence between the purpose of observing and the nature of the categories. Thus the proper application of interaction analysis begins by identifying the purposes of observation clearly and then designing a set of categories that fits the purposes. Only rarely will an existing set of categories be appropriate."[5]

---

[2]For information regarding numerous systems and for a consideration of various aspects of classroom observation, see D. M. Medley and H. E. Mitzel, "Measuring Classroom Behavior by Systematic Observation," in N. L. Gage, *Handbook of Research on Teaching* (Chicago: Rand-McNally, 1963), pp. 247–328.

[3]Edmund Amidon and Ned A. Flanders, *The Role of the Teacher in the Classroom* (Philadelphia: Group Dynamics Center, Temple University, 1962), p. 5.

[4]The categories have been adapted from Ned A. Flanders, *Interaction Analysis in the Classroom: A Manual for Observers* (rev. ed.; Ann Arbor: University of Michigan School of Education, 1964), p. 5.

[5]*Ibid.,* p. 30.

# TOOL 13

Outline of Interaction Analysis

TEACHER TALK--INDIRECT INFLUENCE

1. Accepts feelings: accepts and clarifies the feelings of the pupils in a nonthreatening manner. Feelings may be positive or negative. Predicting or recalling feelings are included.

2. Praises or encourages: praises or encourages pupil action or behavior. Jokes that release tension, but not at the expense of another individual, as well as nodding head or saying "um-hm" or "go on" are included.

3. Accepts or uses ideas of pupil: clarifies or develops ideas suggested by a pupil. As the teacher brings more of his own ideas into play, shift to Category 5.

4. Asks questions: asks a question about content or procedure with the intent that a pupil answer.

TEACHER TALK--DIRECT INFLUENCE

5. Lecturing: gives facts or opinions about content or procedures; expresses his own ideas; asks rhetorical questions.

6. Giving directions: directs, commands, or orders with the intent that pupils comply.

7. Criticizing or justifying authority: makes statements intended to change pupil behavior from nonacceptable to acceptable pattern; criticizes or rebukes; states why he is doing what he is doing; refers extensively to himself.

STUDENT TALK

8. Response: pupil makes a predictable response to teacher. Teacher initiates the contact or solicits pupil's statement and sets limits to what the pupil says. Shift from 8 to 9 as pupil introduces own ideas.

9. Initiation: a pupil initiates communication with the teacher including unpredictable statements in response to teacher.

UNDIRECTED ACTIVITY

10. Silence or confusion: pauses, short periods of silence, and periods of confusion in which communication cannot be understood by the observer.

Teachers should feel free to change categories or develop new ones to meet their particular needs, although experience has shown that the categories in Tool 13 can be used in a majority of classroom situations.

About every three seconds the observer decides which category best represents the communication just completed. He writes down the category number while simultaneously assessing communication during the next period, and continues at a rate of twenty to twenty-five observations per minute, keeping his tempo as steady as possible. His notes are merely a sequence of numbers written in a column, top to bottom, preserving the original sequence of events. He may use occasional marginal notes to explain the class formation—the physical organization of the pupils—or any unusual circumstances. When there is a major change in class formation, communication pattern, or subject under discussion, he draws a double line and indicates the time. At the end of an observed session the observer writes a brief description of each separate activity period indicated by the double lines, including the nature of the activities, the class formation, and the position of the teacher. He also notes any additional facts that seem pertinent to an adequate interpretation and recall of the session. Tool 12 could be modified to accommodate such additional information also.

As stated by Flanders, the system is simple, but some preparation is needed to obtain accurate data. The first step is to memorize the categories; the second step is to practice using them. Categorizing statements from tape recordings of various teaching situations is excellent practice.

At times an observer may need help in making subtle distinctions between categories. The following ground rules have been found useful in developing consistency of observation.

1. When not certain in which of two or more categories a statement belongs, choose the category that is numerically furthest from Category 5.
2. If the primary tone of the teacher's behavior has been consistently direct or consistently indirect, do not shift into the opposite classification unless a clear indication of shift is given by the teacher.
3. The observer must not be concerned with his own biases or with the teacher's intent.
4. If more than one category occurs during the three-second interval, then all categories used in that interval are recorded; or, conversely, each change in category is recorded. If no change occurs within three seconds, repeat that category number.
5. If a silence is long enough for a break in the interaction to be discernible, and if it occurs at a three-second recording time, it is recorded as a 10.[6]

---

[6]Amidon and Flanders, *op. cit.,* pp. 21–24. Pages 15–21 provide further aids in differentiating between categories.

Observational data obtained by means of the Flanders system indicate not only how often each type of behavior occurred but also the sequence of other behaviors within which it occurred. From them the teacher and the observer may be able to construct a general pattern of possible behavioral cause and effect. The teacher can determine how direct or indirect he is by comparing the number of times his actions fall in Categories 1 through 4 (indirect) with those in 5 through 7 (direct). He can check his pupils' responses to each of his actions by the frequency with which either Category 8 or 9 follows his particular action. He is likely to find, for example, that pupil-initiated responses follow indirect influences more often than direct, and that his behavior in Category 3 as a reaction to pupil responses encourages even more pupil participation, falling especially in Category 9.

A comparison of his behavior in Categories 2 and 7 will reveal a teacher's proportionate use of criticism and praise. Sequences of 3 and 9 will indicate his ability to build on what a pupil has presented or to evoke pupil-initiated statements. The silence or confusion as he presents new ideas to the class will show up in behaviors classed as 10.

In studying the observational data from a particular classroom, it may be of interest to compare it with some general research findings. Flanders has found, for example, that in the average classroom someone is talking two-thirds of the time. Two-thirds of this time it is the teacher who is talking; and two-thirds of the time the teacher is talking, he is using direct influence. On the average, then, 67 percent of the observational tallies would be "teacher talks," or Categories 1 through 7; and 30 percent of all activity would fall into Categories 5 through 7.[7] Other investigators have reported similar findings.

## Case Studies in Classroom Observation

I. A fifth-grade teacher, concerned about the effects on her pupils of her way of teaching, assessed the general classroom learning climate by using some of the tools presented in Chapter Two. She was surprised to discover that many of the pupils did not feel involved in the subject matter and were not clear about what she expected of them.

She mustered up courage and asked a colleague to observe her during a teaching hour. The principal was amenable to the plan and willing to fill in for the colleague while she observed the teacher. The teachers decided to use the first observation method described above (Tools 11 and 12).

---

[7]*Ibid.,* p. 43.

After the first hour it was clear to the observer that the fifth-grade teacher spent most of the session telling and giving information to the whole class (Category I-A-1 in the outline). The observer felt that everything was clearly stated and presented, but she saw that many of the pupils were not following. The observer recommended that the teacher address individuals more often, using both direct and indirect probing to reinforce key points and to get continuing feedback on the effectiveness of her communication.

Another observation was that the teacher addressed girls more often than boys, who consequently were left out and played around more than the teacher realized. A check on the data the teacher had collected previously from Tools 2 and 4 indicated that the boys were much less involved and less motivated than the girls.

The teacher now tried actively to involve and to motivate more pupils. She called on individuals more than she had in the past and was more conscious of her reactions to boys in the class. She also had the pupils work in small groups at times so that each of them would have a greater opportunity to participate in classroom work.

After several weeks she asked her colleague to observe her performance once again. It was clear to the observer that changes had occurred along the lines that the teacher had laid down for herself. At the end of the hour the observer used Tools 4 and 10 to gather data from the pupils on their reactions to the learning task. These data indicated that the pupils were much more involved, more attracted to classroom tasks, and more excited about their academic learning than the earlier data had shown.

About a week later the observer approached the teacher and asked to be observed. She had been impressed by the improvement following observation and knew that she, too, could improve in certain areas of teaching. Observation and feedback had been both helpful and contagious.

II. A high school English teacher felt that the academic involvement of his students was very low in most of his classes and he was concerned about his students' inability to retain the content they had studied earlier in the course. After talking with colleagues, he held class discussions with students on what would help them in retaining their studies and began to plan a curriculum sequence in collaboration with them. Despite these efforts, class morale, involvement in studies, and retention of content did not increase appreciably. Somewhat frustrated, the teacher asked a colleague to observe several of his classroom planning sessions. They decided to use Flanders' interaction analysis during these sessions.

Two hours of classroom observation produced several enlightening results. The observer found that the teacher was interacting mostly in

Categories 5 (lecturing), 4 (asks questions), and 6 (giving directions). Student comments fell largely into category 8 (response). One pattern of interaction occurred frequently: the sequence 4 (asking questions), 8 (student response), a series of 5s (lecturing), and back to 4 again. In brief, the teacher raised questions about ways of approaching the next week's academic work, and the students responded to these questions with their ideas; thereupon the teacher dropped the student's ideas and presented his own approach by lecturing. The teacher's behaviors seldom fell into Category 1 (accepts feeling), 2 (praises or encourages), or 3 (accepts or uses ideas of student); and the pupils hardly ever presented their own thoughts spontaneously (9). Category 10 (silence or confusion) occurred with increasing frequency toward the end of each observation period.

The observer and the teacher discussed these results at length. At first the teacher found them very difficult to understand and tried to find fault with the categories. These difficulties might have been averted had the teacher and the observer thoroughly outlined their objectives beforehand and evaluated the categories in relation to them. Gradually the teacher overcame his defensive attitude and began to understand how his teaching behaviors were actively defeating his teaching objectives and leading to low student involvement. Although he made some effort to elicit creative responses from students, his subsequent actions seemed to indicate that he was primarily interested in developing his own ideas rather than those offered by the students. The students were thus increasingly frustrated in their attempts to contribute effectively to the learning situation.

Subsequently the teacher tried hard to accept feelings and ideas from the students and to praise and encourage them. He had difficulty in presenting a revised image of himself to these students, however, because of their well-established expectations of his behavior. Not until the next semester, with a new class, was he able to put his insights fully into practice.

# CHAPTER SIX

# Outside Influences
# on Pupil Learning

The preceding four chapters have dealt with the teacher's diagnosis of the social and psychological relations that contribute, positively or negatively, to classroom learning atmospheres. But the school is only one of the many forces acting on the pupil's life: what he does in school obviously depends on more than the events in the classroom or those activities in his day that are in some measure controlled by the school. The values, expectations, and ways of behaving accepted by significant others in the child's world will in part constitute the field of forces within which the teacher hopes to exert influence. Each of the forces illustrated in Fig. 5 will in varying degrees shape the child's personality and behavior. This chapter and the two succeeding ones assume the necessity, if the teacher's influences are to be purposefully and positively directed, of working to compensate for negative forces that exist outside the classroom.

The teacher's job is not, of course, to launch a direct attack on problems that may be a part of the child's out-of-school environment, since many of these will lie in areas that he cannot approach ethically. Furthermore, the teacher should be aware that the types of questions in these three chapters are often highly sensitive to parental and community opinion. He should consider the suggestions in Chapter One that he carefully outline and be prepared to explain his objectives and that he have firm administrative support for his activities.

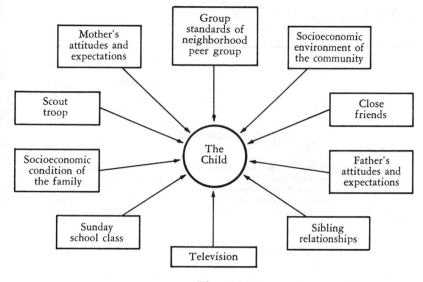

**Fig. 5**

SOME FORCES THAT INFLUENCE THE CHILD

## Gathering Information About Out-of-School Life

Teachers concerned with improving a child's motivation for learning may want to gather data on such questions as these:

- What is the importance of school for the child among the activities within his total day?
- What is the importance of the teacher compared with other persons in the pupil's life?
- What attitudes about education and about the school does the child gain from his family and from his neighborhood?
- What activities in the pupil's out-of-school life may be competing with school-centered activities for his time, energy, and emotional commitment?

Some information about a pupil's home background can be gathered from school records, which should be utilized whenever possible so that classroom time can be used to gather information that is more difficult to obtain. Each pupil can supply data on Tool 14 during the beginning days of school.

## TOOL 14

GETTING ACQUAINTED WITH YOU

Your teacher needs to know more about you. The answers you give to the questions on this paper will help him to get acquainted with you. We will not talk about your answers in class. You can answer some questions by making a circle around either YES or NO. You can write your answers to other questions on the blank lines following the questions.

1. Write your name, address, and telephone number.

   Name _____

   Address _____

   Telephone number _____

2. If you have brothers or sisters--

   a. Write the names of your brothers:

      _____ How old? _____

      _____ How old? _____

      _____ How old? _____

   b. Write the names of your sisters:

      _____ How old? _____

      _____ How old? _____

      _____ How old? _____

3. If any of your brothers or sisters have grown up and left home, put a circle around their age in Question 2.

4. Which of the people listed below live with your family? (Please check)

   _____ Mother

   _____ Father

   _____ Stepmother

---

_____ Stepfather

_____ Other adults

All together, how many adults live with you? _____

5. Does a sitter stay with you when your mother and father are away
   from home?     YES     NO

   a.  If yes, is it the same person all the time?          YES          NO

   b.  If yes, is it someone in your family?          YES          NO

   c.  If yes, who is it? _____

---

Many children have to make frequent adjustments to a new school because their families have moved. Information about previous school attendance can be obtained by adding the following item.

---

6. Think back to the time when you first started going to school. In
   the blanks below, write the name of the city or town and the state
   where you went to school at each grade that you have finished so
   far. If you did not change for two or more years, use ditto marks
   to show that it was the same city or town and state.
   Did you go to kindergarten?   YES    NO    If you did not, skip the
   line marked kindergarten and start with the first grade.

   | Grade | City or Town | State |
   |-------|--------------|-------|
   | Kindergarten | | |
   | First grade | | |
   | Second grade | | |
   | Third grade | | |
   | etc. | | |

---

Other children may have jobs after school. For some this is a constructive opportunity for developing responsibility and becoming independent. For others, the out-of-school work may be a heavy burden, restricting opportunities for interaction with peers, interfering with study, or creating physical fatigue. Such questions as the following may be added to gain information about these matters.

67

## TOOL 14 (continued)

7. What regular duties do you have at home other than jobs for which
   you are paid? _____

   _____

   _____

8. Do you have a job or do part-time work for pay?

   YES    NO

   a. If yes, please check:

   _____ Under 5 hours a week, average

   _____ 5 to 9 hours a week, average

   _____ 10 to 14 hours a week, average

   _____ 15 to 19 hours a week, average

   _____ 20 or more hours a week, average

   b. If yes, do you work

   _____ for your family?

   _____ for someone else?

   _____ for both family and someone else?

   c. If for someone else, please give the name of your employer.

   _____

   d. What, exactly, do you do on your job? _____

   _____

   e. What hours do you work? _____

   _____

   _____

The Getting Acquainted with You instrument may very well include some of the questions about parents that are presented in the next chapter, "Parental Influences on School Adjustment."

Data that go beyond the objective facts may help the teacher to understand the out-of-school forces that influence the child. Since the child acts on the basis of his perceptions, knowing the relative importance to him of the several forces in his life is valuable. Tool 15 might serve such a purpose.

## TOOL 15

Date _____

Your number _____

Class _____

PARTS OF YOUR DAY

A day has several different parts, in which you do different things.
Some parts of the day seem more important to you than the other parts.

Which part of your day seems most important to you?

Put a number 1 in the column under "Importance" beside the part of the
day that seems most important to you. Then put a 2 beside the part of
the day that seems next most important to you. Put a 3 beside the part
of the day that seems next most important; a 4 beside the next; a 5 beside the next; and a 6 beside the part of the day that seems least important to you. There are no right or wrong answers.

                                                       Importance

Life in this class     _____

Life in other classes     _____

Things you do in school that are
not part of your regular classes     _____

Life at home     _____

Doing things with playmates
after school     _____

Clubs and groups outside school with
regular meetings and adult leaders     _____

Doing things alone     _____

The Parts of Your Day instrument can be modified to explore other dimensions of the pupil's feelings about the forces in his life. Questions might be phrased "In which part of your day do you feel happiest?" or "In which part of the day do you feel you are learning the most things?"

Another way to study the pupil's feeling about the life-space forces that affect him is to ask him how he would alter, if he could, the amount of time he spends in these various settings.

The items in Tools 15 and 16 are written for elementary school children; an adaptation for secondary school students might include the following items:

69

1. Life in this class
2. Life in other classes
3. Other school activities that are not classes
4. Life at home
5. Social life with friends—on our own, away from home and school
6. Clubs and groups outside school with regular meetings and adult leaders
7. Doing things alone

## TOOL 16

Date _____

Your number _____

Class _____

### CHANGING THE PARTS OF YOUR DAY

Let's imagine you could change some of the things you do during the day. Put a check in the box that shows how you would change the parts of your day. There are no right or wrong answers.

|  | A lot more time | Some more time | A little less time | A lot less time |
|---|---|---|---|---|
| 1. Life in this class |  |  |  |  |
| 2. Life in other classes |  |  |  |  |
| 3. Things you do in school that are not part of your regular classes |  |  |  |  |
| 4. Life at home |  |  |  |  |
| 5. Doing things with playmates after school |  |  |  |  |
| 6. Clubs and groups outside school with regular meetings and adult leaders |  |  |  |  |
| 7. Doing things alone |  |  |  |  |

Tools 15 and 16 focus on the child's life situations. A parallel type of instrument to focus on the people who are a part of the child's life is presented in Tool 17.

## TOOL 17

Date _____

Your number _____

Class _____

TALKING WITH PEOPLE

During a day or week you spend a great deal of time talking with various people both in and out of school. Here is a list of some of the people in your life. Some of these people you talk with more than others, and you often talk about different things.

Which people do you talk to about the most important things? Put a number 1 in the column under "Importance" beside the name of the person(s) with whom you talk about the most important things. Then put a 2 beside the name of the person(s) with whom you talk about the next most important things. Put a 3 for the next person(s); a 4 for the next: a 5 for the next: and a 6 for the person(s) with whom you talk about the least important things. There are no right or wrong answers.

|  | Importance |
|---|---|
| My close friend(s) in this class | _____ |
| Others in this class | _____ |
| My mother | _____ |
| Friend(s) not in this class | _____ |
| My father | _____ |
| My teacher(s) | _____ |

This instrument can be adapted to explore other dimensions of the relationship of the pupil with the people in his life. Such questions as "Which people do you *feel happiest with* when you talk with them?" and "Which people do you feel you *learn most from* by talking with them?" would be appropriate.

In addition to finding out the relative importance of the various people and periods in the pupil's life space, the teacher may wish to ascertain the reactions of some of these people to the kind of work the child is doing in school. The general question "How satisfied are they?" might be asked as in Tool 18.

Some very interesting information can come from asking the child whether he feels the important people in his life think of him in positive or in negative terms as in Tool 19.

## TOOL 18

Date _____

Your number _____

Class _____

### HOW SATISFIED ARE THEY?

Put a check in the box that tells how satisfied you think each one of these people is with your schoolwork. There are no right or wrong answers.

| | Very satis-fied | Pretty well satis-fied | Not well satis-fied | Not sat-isfied at all | Don't really care |
|---|---|---|---|---|---|
| 1. My close friend(s) in this class | | | | | |
| 2. Others in this class | | | | | |
| 3. My mother | | | | | |
| 4. Friends not in this class | | | | | |
| 5. The teacher in this class | | | | | |
| 6. My father | | | | | |
| 7. How satisfied am I with myself? | | | | | |

## *Recording and Analyzing the Data*

Much of the information gathered about the out-of-school influences on the pupil's life will be useful to the teacher in working with the individual child rather than with the group. For example, the completed Tool 14, Getting Acquainted with You, would probably be filed by the teacher for future reference, and this and other forms could provide valuable insights into the results of other diagnostic measures made during the school year. If the teacher finds it valuable, a frequency count of responses to such questions as out-of-school work or number of different schools attended can give some notion of the importance of these forces upon the

# TOOL 19

Date _____

Your number _____

Class _____

HOW THEY SEE ME

Just as each part of the day is filled with positive, neutral, and negative things, each person is made up of things we like and things we do not like so much. Below are a number of circles showing persons with different amounts of positive (+) and negative (-) things about them. Which of these circles comes closest to the way you see yourself? Write the letter of the circle which most resembles you right here: _____ .

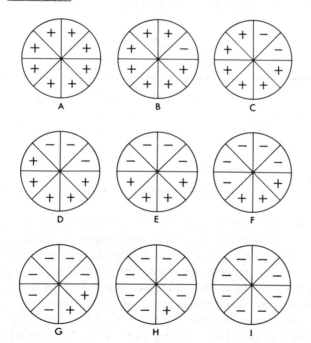

In the blank following each question, write the letter of the circle that you think each of the persons mentioned would pick for you.

1. Which circle do you think your closest friend would choose to describe you? _____

2. Which circle would the teacher in this class choose? _____

---

3. Which circle would the principal of your school choose? _____

4. Which circle would your mother choose? _____

5. Which circle would the boys or girls you spend most time with choose to describe you? _____

6. Which circle would your father choose? _____

---

class as a whole. Tools 15 and 17, Parts of Your Day and Talking with People, can be interpreted more easily if the individual response can be compared with the class average.

One high school teacher accomplished this by preparing the overall tally sheet of responses shown in Table 7.

### Table 7

SUMMARY OF "Parts of Your Day"

|  | 1 | 2 | 3 | 4 | 5 | 6 | 7 |
|---|---|---|---|---|---|---|---|
| 1. Life in this class | 3 | 6 | 3 | 2 | 2 | 3 | 1 |
| 2. Life in other classes | 0 | 2 | 4 | 4 | 3 | 3 | 4 |
| 3. Other school activities | 2 | 1 | 4 | 6 | 2 | 4 | 1 |
| 4. Life at home | 3 | 4 | 3 | 2 | 2 | 3 | 3 |
| 5. Social life with friends | 5 | 4 | 3 | 1 | 6 | 1 | 0 |
| 6. Clubs and groups outside school | 2 | 0 | 1 | 4 | 2 | 3 | 8 |
| 7. Doing things alone | 5 | 3 | 2 | 1 | 3 | 3 | 3 |

He was then able to draw several conclusions about his class. First, individual pupils varied considerably with regard to which parts of the day ranked high or low in importance. For example, three pupils ranked "life at home" of greatest importance; three ranked it of less importance than all other aspects of their life space included in the instrument. Five pupils considered "doing things alone" of highest importance; three considered it of least importance. Further, "social life with friends" seemed to be of special importance to many in the class. Very few of the pupils in this class considered it unimportant.

"Life in this class" ranked as an important part of the pupils' total life. Moreover, "life in this class" was considered somewhat more important than that in other class periods in the school day. This information may reflect the true state of affairs, or it may be that pupils responded favorably to please the teacher. The teacher will therefore want to be somewhat cautious in his interpretation of these data. He might try to collaborate with other teachers in the school who have these same pupils in class, interesting them in a parallel study of the learning climate.

This teacher discovered more about the state of affairs by analyzing the results of the Changing the Parts of Your Day questionnaire. He tallied it as shown in Table 8:

It appeared that although many pupils ranked "life in this class" of high importance relative to other parts of their day, almost no one in the class would want to see more time given to the class activities. They would like to increase the time available for independent social life, nonclass school activities, and life at home. This apparent dissatisfaction with the state of affairs in the classroom may be a normal reaction to the "work" part of the day. On the other hand, it is interesting to examine the summary made by another teacher in the same school as shown in Table 9: although the desire to increase time spent in some other aspects of the day existed in both classes, in this second class more than one-third of the pupils would like to increase the time spent "in this class."

### Table 8

SUMMARY OF "Changing the Parts of Your Day"—CLASS 1

| | A lot more time | Some more time | Same time as now | Little less time | A lot less time | No time at all |
|---|---|---|---|---|---|---|
| 1. Life in this class | 1 | 1 | 14 | 3 | 1 | 0 |
| 2. Life in other classes | 1 | 4 | 8 | 4 | 2 | 1 |
| 3. Other school activities that are not classes | 9 | 2 | 4 | 2 | 1 | 2 |
| 4. Life at home | 6 | 4 | 5 | 3 | 0 | 2 |
| 5. Social life with friends | 12 | 6 | 2 | 0 | 0 | 0 |
| 6. Clubs and groups outside school | 3 | 3 | 8 | 1 | 2 | 3 |
| 7. Doing things alone | 1 | 1 | 16 | 2 | 0 | 0 |

### Table 9

SUMMARY OF "Changing the Parts of Your Day"—CLASS 2

| | A lot more time | Some more time | Same time as now | Little less time | A lot less time | No time at all |
|---|---|---|---|---|---|---|
| 1. Life in this class | 3 | 4 | 8 | 3 | 2 | 0 |
| 2. Life in other classes | 1 | 7 | 6 | 4 | 1 | 1 |
| 3. Other school activities that are not classes | 7 | 3 | 5 | 3 | 0 | 2 |
| 4. Life at home | 3 | 6 | 7 | 2 | 1 | 1 |
| 5. Social life with friends | 10 | 7 | 3 | 0 | 0 | 0 |
| 6. Clubs and groups outside school | 4 | 3 | 6 | 1 | 3 | 3 |
| 7. Doing things alone | 0 | 4 | 15 | 1 | 0 | 0 |

Another teacher found some clues about the home pressures on his pupils' academic work by analyzing the data from Tool 18, How Satisfied Are They? (see Table 10).

It appears that the mothers and fathers are considerably more anxious than the teacher about their son's or daughter's performance; mothers tend to be seen as more dissatisfied than fathers. The average pupil perceives the pressures for academic performance as coming from home more than from the teacher. He is not as satisfied with his own performance as he thinks the teacher is. He sees his close friends as being more satisfied than he himself is, but not to the extent the teacher is.

### Table 10

SUMMARY OF "How Satisfied Are They?"

|  | Very satis- fied | Pretty well satis- fied | Not well satis- fied | Not satis- fied at all | Don't really care |
|---|---|---|---|---|---|
| 1. My close friend(s) in this class | 9 | 6 | 2 | 1 | 2 |
| 2. Others in this class | 4 | 5 | 3 | 2 | 6 |
| 3. My mother | 2 | 5 | 9 | 4 | 0 |
| 4. Friends *not* in this class | 3 | 4 | 1 | 0 | 12 |
| 5. The teacher in this class | 11 | 4 | 3 | 2 | 0 |
| 6. My father | 3 | 7 | 6 | 3 | 1 |
| 7. How satisfied am I with myself? | 7 | 9 | 3 | 1 | 0 |

Again, these data can take on more significance with the discovery that similar conditions do not necessarily exist in other classrooms.

Such knowledge about some of the pressures and influences that the various parts of each pupil's life exert on his classroom behavior can help the teacher plan an effective educational experience for every pupil. With such information the teacher can show the pupils that he understands their individual situations. Further, if "facts" obtained by the teacher and the way these "facts" are perceived by the pupil are incongruent, and if the teacher feels the pupil's perceptions are in error, he may be able to help make these perceptions more realistic. For example, discrepancies that exist between a child's school performance as the teacher knows it to be and the way the child thinks it is perceived by his parents can be thoroughly discussed in a three-way conference of parents, pupil, and teacher, possibly after the teacher has sought such additional data on parental influences as the following chapter describes.

# CHAPTER SEVEN

# Parental Influences
# on School Adjustment

Teachers know well the important effect of home conditions and parental attitudes on the child. They have found repeatedly that when the values of the family and the school are contradictory, the pupil's schoolwork suffers. If a child feels that his parents do not care about his school life, he, too, is unlikely to care and consequently may become an underachiever and a behavior problem in the classroom.[1]

The young child's early adjustments to the learning atmosphere may come to characterize his entire school career and eventually his own influences as a parent. The longer poor adjustments are allowed to persist, the more difficult they will be to change. Since parental attitudes are so crucial to positive school adjustment, the teacher should seek information about his pupils' families—about these attitudes and values that have been so significant in forming the child's approach to life. This is especially important at the start of the school year with a new group of pupils.

## Methods of Obtaining Information

The teacher may ask himself a number of questions about a pupil's homelife.

- What persons live in the home with the pupil?
- What kind of work does the father do?
- Is the mother employed outside the home? If she is, what kind of work does she do?

---

[1]M. B. Luszki and R. Schmuck, "Pupil Perceptions of Parental Attitudes Toward School," *Mental Hygiene,* 49, No. 2 (April 1965), 296–307.

- Is anyone at home when the child returns from school? If so, who?
- What magazines, newspapers, and books are in the home?
- What does the child do when he gets home from school?
- When and under what conditions does he do his homework? Does his mother or his father ever help him or offer to help?
- Are excessive demands made upon his time that interfere with schoolwork or with needed play activities?

Much information about the home background and influences can be obtained through informal contacts with pupils and parents, and some factual material can usually be obtained from school records. Teachers who have the time may even wish to visit some of the homes. But it is often desirable to use some special tools to obtain from all the pupils as clear a picture as possible of the parents' influences on school adjustment.

To supplement the general information about his pupils, the teacher might add a number of questions about parents and homelife to Tool 14, Getting Acquainted with You, shown in the preceding chapter. For example, information about the father's occupation, in addition to its direct interest, gives a fairly reliable estimate of the family's socioeconomic level. To be most useful, however, the data must be gathered more carefully than by simply asking "What does your father do?" The following series of questions may be helpful.

## TOOL 14 (continued)

9. Where does your father work? _____

10. What is the name or title of his job? _____
_____

11. Does he have a boss or supervisor?          YES     NO

    Does he supervise, or is he in charge of the work of other people?                              YES     NO

                          If yes, about how many? _____

12. What exactly does he do on the job? _____
_____
_____

With many mothers employed away from the home, it is often important to learn something about the mother's occupation. Such questions as the following may serve.

---

13. Does your mother have a job in addition to taking care of your
    home?                                    YES        NO

    If your answer is yes, please answer the following:

    a.  Does she work full or part time?
        (Please check)

        _____  She works full time.
        _____  She works part time.

    b.  Where does she work? _____

        _____

    c.  What is the name of her job? _____

        _____

    d.  What exactly does she do on the job? _____

        _____

14. Is your mother usually at home when you get home from school?
                                    YES        NO

    If she is not, is some other adult there when you get home from
    school?                         YES        NO

    Who? _____

---

At times a teacher may want to categorize occupational information to get an overall picture of the class or to compare it with other classes. The literature contains many different occupational scales, or classifications, but despite attempts to define the categories objectively, discrimination between some of them is often difficult. Classification is frequently a matter of judgment, and rather detailed questions, such as those above, may be needed for a correct judgment.

Occupational scales contain from three categories to fourteen or more, depending upon the purpose and the degree of refinement desired. Some investigators use U.S. Census Bureau categories; other develop categories to suit their particular needs. For most classroom purposes a classification of occupations into three major categories is sufficient. With a more detailed breakdown, the few cases in most of the categories make the finer classifications of little value. The following categorization has been found useful in analyzing particular classrooms and in comparing class-rooms.

I. Jobs requiring extensive training and experience and involving heavy responsibility: persons in professions that require at least four years of college; proprietors, managers, and others in high positions of responsibility in large business and industry; high-ranking public officials; and the like.

II. Jobs requiring a moderate amount of training or technical skills and abilities: semiprofessional personnel, such as those in fields requiring two years of college or specialized education; proprietors and office managers of small businesses; most white-collar workers; police and firemen; skilled mechanics (journeyman level); farmers; and the like.

III. Jobs requiring little or no training or experience: semiskilled and unskilled workers; persons in lower-level clerical and sales jobs, such as grocery store clerks and shipping clerks; helpers to skilled craftsmen; assembly-line workers; day laborers; domestic help; and the like.

The educational level of parents is also of interest. It is often closely related to occupational status, but in many cases the combination of occupational and educational information gives a much better picture of the parents than either kind of information alone. The following questions may elicit educational information in a useful form.

---

15. How far did your father go in school? (Please check)

_____ Attended 8 years of school or less

_____ Attended from 9 to 11 years of school

_____ Graduated from high school

_____ Went to college: How many years? _____

_____ Graduated from college

_____ Went to school beyond college

_____ Don't know

16. How far did your mother go in school? (Please check)

_____ Attended 8 years of school or less

_____ Attended from 9 to 11 years of school

_____ Graduated from high school

_____ Went to college: How many years? _____

_____ Graduated from college

_____ Went to school beyond college

_____ Don't know

## Subjective Pupil Evaluations of the Home Environment

To get a pupil's view of his home situation, in-class compositions on such subjects as "My Day" or "A Day at Home" are often useful. Teachers who have done this successfully accompany the assignment with specific items and questions, which would vary with the grade level and the particular information the teacher would like to obtain. The following outline suggests a number of aspects of the home situation, any one of which might be used for a short English composition.

1. My family
   a. Who are the people who live at home with you? Tell something about them.
   b. Whom do you talk with most at home? What kinds of things do you talk about?
2. Our house
   a. Tell something about your house.
   b. What do you do to help take care of it? Do you have any chores or responsibilities around the house or yard?
   c. Where do you sleep? Do you have any roommates? Who?
   d. Where do you study? Who else is in the room with you when you are studying?
3. Getting up in the morning
   a. Do you like to get up?
   b. When do you get up?
   c. Do you wake up on your own, or does somebody wake you? Who? How do you feel when you first get up?
   d. How long does it take you to get dressed?
   e. Who fixes breakfast?

**81**

      f. What do you usually have for breakfast? What is your favorite breakfast?

4. Schooltime
   a. When do you leave home for school?
   b. How do you get to school?
   c. Tell something about your day in school.

5. After school
   a. Where do you usually go after school? How do you get there?
   b. With whom do you usually do things? What do you do?
   c. About what time do you usually get home?
   d. Who is usually at home when you get there?
   e. What do you like best after school?

6. Homework
   a. Do you have homework most of the time? If you do, about how much time do you have to spend on it?
   b. Where do you do it?
   c. When do you do it?
   d. What are other people in the family doing when you are studying? Are any of them in the same room with you?
   e. Are there books or magazines in the house that help you with your studies?

7. Evening and bedtime
   a. What TV programs do you watch? Which do you like best? Why?
   b. What else do you do in the evenings?
   c. Do you have books or magazines at home? What kind are they? Which ones do you like to read?
   d. What time do you go to bed on school nights?

The sentence-completion tool discussed in Chapter Nine provides another means of obtaining a child's impressions and attitudes about many areas of his life. The following two sentence stems in particular give valuable qualitative information on the way a child perceives his parents' attitudes toward school. The contrasting completions obtained from two pupils suggest the kinds of responses that can be expected.

When I talk about school, my mother *(is always helpful) (asks how many bad things did you do in school)*.

When I talk about school, my father *(is proud of me) (says he is not interested)*.

Not only do such responses show whether the parents' attitudes are seen as positive or negative, but also they may reveal more subtle feelings about the parents' orientation to school. Some children, for example, see their parents primarily as giving affective support and approval, others as offering help, still others as emphasizing academic achievement. A few see them as threat-oriented, with pressure for improvement of grades—or else!

Quantitatively, the replies lend themselves to rating on a scale ranging from strong approval, affective support, and interest in what the pupil has to say about school ("says I'm doing fine," "is pleased with my schoolwork," "enjoys hearing about school") to a relatively neutral attitude ("sometimes listens," "doesn't mind," "is sometimes interested, sometimes not") to a clearly negative, hostile attitude ("gets mad," "complains about the money I need to get an education," "says I'm not going to pass").

Pupils often complete other sentence stems in a way that throws further light on parental attitudes. In one classroom the stem "If I should fail in school _____" elicited a large number of completions anticipating the consequences at home of such an event. These indicated that the parents "would be very mad" or "disappointed," that they would withdraw privileges or administer other kinds of punishment, or that they would force remedial action, as "my parents would make me work harder than ever." Other stems scattered throughout the tool have been designed to reveal something about the child's relationship with each parent, his place in the family, and the conditions under which he is happiest.

## A Case Study in Data Analysis and Action

One sixth-grade teacher who administered the forty-six sentence stems in Chapter Nine used the responses for an overall qualitative study of the children as persons. She was careful not to draw definite conclusions, recognizing the danger of projecting her own feelings into the sentence completions, of reading too much into them. Yet she felt these responses increased her understanding of her pupils.

### Recording and Analyzing the Data

She decided to make a separate quantitative tabulation of the completions of the two stems "When I talk about school, my mother (father) _____." First she made her own evaluation of whether each child's parents were positive (+), neutral (0), or negative (−) in their attitudes toward school, basing her judgment on whatever information was available to her—contacts with the parents themselves, school records, experience with older siblings, comments by other teachers, and the like. Next she coded the pupil's completions for each parent, using the same scale and symbols. Finally she entered the pupil's achievement level as she knew it, high (H) or low (L), for comparison with parental attitudes. Table 11 is the completed summary for her twenty-five pupils.

83

## Table 11

### PARENTAL ATTITUDES AND PUPIL ACHIEVEMENT

| Pupil Number | My evaluation of parents interest in school | *SENTENCE COMPLETION DATA* Pupil's perceived attitude of: | | Pupil's achievement level |
|---|---|---|---|---|
| | | Mother | Father | |
| 1 | − | 0 | − | L |
| 2 | + | + | + | H |
| 3 | − | + | + | H |
| 4 | + | + | + | H |
| 5 | 0 | + | 0 | L |
| 6 | + | + | + | H |
| 7 | − | 0 | 0 | L |
| 8 | 0 | + | + | H |
| 9 | − | 0 | 0 | L |
| 10 | − | 0 | + | L |
| 11 | + | − | 0 | L |
| 12 | − | + | 0 | L |
| 13 | + | + | 0 | H |
| 14 | 0 | + | + | H |
| 15 | + | − | + | H |
| 16 | + | + | + | H |
| 17 | + | − | − | L |
| 18 | + | + | 0 | L |
| 19 | − | 0 | 0 | L |
| 20 | − | + | + | L |
| 21 | + | + | − | H |
| 22 | − | 0 | 0 | L |
| 23 | + | + | + | H |
| 24 | − | + | no father | L |
| 25 | 0 | + | 0 | L |

Although many more parents were seen by the pupils as supportive of school than nonsupportive, there were some who were clearly seen as negative and a fair number who fell in the neutral category. Moreover, some families were split, with the mother supportive and the father not, or vice versa.

In going over her table, the teacher found that she had completely misjudged the parents of Pupils 11 and 17. Both couples were themselves well educated and seemed very school-oriented; they had told her they expected their children to go to college. She had rated them plus. Yet the children had completed the sentences in ways such as "my mother says she is too busy to talk to me now" and "my father keeps on reading the newspaper." This discrepancy—between the parents' avowed interest in school and the child's perception of lack of interest—brought to the teacher's mind some research that had shown that a child's conception of his relationship with his parents is not necessarily akin to his parents' view of the same relation. It had shown also that the child's conception of the relationship, rather than the relationship as perceived by the parent or by an outside observer, was a crucial factor in his adjustment.[2] These findings convinced her that she should put more weight on the sentence-completion data than on her evaluation of parents' attitudes. They suggested, too, that she might have to use one kind of strategy with parents whom she had rated positive but whom their children rated negative and another with parents rated negatively by both herself and the pupils.

She also found another kind of discrepancy between her ratings and the attitudes revealed by the sentence completions. The parents of Pupils 3 and 20 had less than an eighth-grade education, and she had judged the parents to have no interest in school; yet the children completed the sentences with such statements as "likes to listen," "wants to know," and "is proud of me." The teacher concluded that she had failed to understand these parents, who came from a background different from her own. Not at all lacking in interest in school, they were primarily awed by it and uncomfortable in the unfamiliar surroundings, yet wanted "school learning" for their children.

One rather disturbing finding was that ten fathers and six mothers were rated neutral on the basis of the sentence-completion response ("listens sometimes," "is only interested sometimes," "says things were different when he went to school"). The teacher felt that these seemingly neutral parents were really negative, that by being uninterested or ambivalent in their attitude toward school they were actually nonsupportive of their child's school life.

## An Action Program

As a guide for future work the teacher made what she headed "Exploration and/or Remedial-Action List," with pupils' names grouped in the following categories.

Mother supportive, father neutral or negative
(Pupils 5, 12, 13, 18, 21, 25)
Father supportive, mother neutral or negative
(Pupils 10, 15)
Both parents neutral or negative
(Pupils 1, 7, 9, 11, 17, 19, 22)

Her list had fifteen names, a surprising number in a community she had considered school-oriented. It was a rather alarming discovery, for the teacher was aware of research showing that pupils who feel their parents are interested in and supportive of their school life make a more positive

---

[2]N. M. Serot and R. C. Teevan, "Perception of the Parent-Child Relationship and Its Relation to Child Adjustment," *Child Development*, 32 (June 1961), 373-78.

adjustment to school than do pupils who perceive less parental support, particularly in the lower grades.[3]

The teacher headed the list as she did because she felt her first step was further exploration. She could not judge a home on the basis of a child's response to two incomplete sentences, but she could and did use these responses to point to where some exploration should be done. She held conferences with parents, made a few home visits, and enlisted the help of the visiting teacher. Where additional information about a home suggested that changes were desirable, she was able in most cases to establish a positive enough relationship with the parents to help them assume more supportive attitudes toward their child's school life.

She also used her material as the basis for a PTA meeting, at which there was a lively discussion of how parents can show interest in the child's school life and what parents can do to let the child know they are interested. The meeting produced many ideas as to how parents can support a child's school endeavors. These were put in the form of questions that parents might ask themselves in order to help evaluate their performance in this area. Three types of support were identified, as indicated in the following list.

1. Intellectual support
   a. Are reading and reference materials available in the home?
   b. Do the parents encourage the child to use them and show him how to do so?
   c. Do parents discuss and share ideas and information?
      (Parents can learn from their children as well as children from their parents.)
2. Emotional support
   a. Are parents easily available to talk with their children when the children want to talk?
   b. Do parents show interest in what the child is doing in school and what he is learning? What are some of the ways to show interest?
3. Social support
   a. Does the child bring his school friends home?
   b. Do parents encourage recreational and "character building" activities, such as little league baseball, school clubs, and other organizations?
   c. Do parents respect the child's rights and his privacy, recognizing his need to be an individual as well as a member of the family?

The teacher found most of the parents eager for information and guidance,

[3]Luszki and Schmuck, *op. cit.*

because their lack of support stemmed largely from their failure to understand child behavior or from their being so busy that they were not aware of the problem.

With one set of parents, she found the negative feelings toward the child and toward school were so deep-rooted that she could not enlist their cooperation. These parents she referred to the visiting teacher, who had special training and more time for such work and could perhaps understand and alleviate the nonsupportive attitudes. The job of understanding and interpretation was clearly a mutual one—to interpret the school to these parents and to interpret these parents to the school. She knew that she had as much to learn in understanding parents of cultural backgrounds different from her own as the parents had in understanding the school. Both she and the visiting teacher recognized that they must not put further pressures and strains on what might already be a difficult home situation. In some extreme cases it might be necessary for the visiting teacher, or the regular teacher if there is no visiting teacher on the school staff, to guide such parents to the appropriate community agency for psychiatric, psychological, or social-service evaluations and help.

As the teacher worked on the problems within her classroom, she knew she could not hope to be fully successful in changing the attitudes of all parents. An alternative action, then, was to help children understand their parents better. Role playing provided a useful tool for helping a child deal with his parents' attitudes toward school, particularly as a springboard for discussion of why parents might not be interested in school and how pupils can help educate their parents.

She also recognized that there are some pupils who like school and do well despite lack of support at home. Many such cases can be attributed to positive child-teacher relationships. Diagnostic findings indicating lack of home support for schoolwork presented her with a dual challenge: (1) to attempt to change the attitudes and behavior of parents through various means and (2) to help compensate, through her work and relations with the children, for negative home influences, so that a child could develop a sense of personal worth and self-fulfillment in the classroom. Not all parents can be changed in the desired direction, and children of such parents present a special challenge to a teacher. If parents are nonsupportive of school, there is a particular need for teacher respect, acceptance, and support. Some educators feel that the teacher can be the "good parent," both in attitudes and in time spent with the child. The main need of such a child is a teacher who will stand by him and respect him as a person, someone on whom he can depend. For a pupil who comes from a cultural background different from the majority of the class, the teacher should try to find the particular skills he has and the contributions he can make because of this background. These can be used to put him in a good light to the other pupils.

Other educators feel that the substitute-parent role is not necessarily the most constructive relationship for a teacher to have with children whose parents are nonsupportive of school. Many children receive ample love and emotional warmth at home despite a lack of understanding of the school and its activities. Consistent and realistic attitudes that are firmly adhered to are important with such children.

These two roles—the teacher as the "good parent" and the teacher who provides a stable, predictable environment—are, in a sense, complementary functions of a good teacher. If the teacher gives the child support and respect, recognizing him as a unique individual, he can go far in overcoming adverse home influences.

# CHAPTER EIGHT

# The Pupil's Concept of Himself

Man's search for an understanding of himself and his efforts to achieve a self that meets certain standards of desirability are probably as old as the human species. In recent years the self has become an object of scientific study as well as of speculative philosophy; many educators and psychologists have recognized it as a concept essential to an understanding of personality. A brief review of some aspects of the self and its development is important for effective use of the tools presented in this chapter.

## The Self-Concept

A self-concept[1] is a person's view of himself, the most complete picture that an individual has of himself at any particular time. In some recent research on the self-concepts of elementary school children, Bledsoe and Garrison refer to the self-concept as "one of the most vital areas of human growth." The authors continue: "An individual's perception of himself may well be the central factor influencing his behavior. . . . The self is involved in social reactions; it operates in the service of need satisfaction, particularly in the enhancement of the self or in relation to self-esteem; it is a vital force in effective adjustment."[2]

---

[1]Although some writers make certain distinctions between *self-concept, self-perception,* and *self-image,* here the terms are used synonymously. Such other terms as *self-esteem* and *self-appraisal* have an added evaluative connotation, and are also used interchangeably.

[2]J. C. Bledsoe and K. C. Garrison, *The Self Concepts of Elementary School Children in Relation to Their Academic Achievement, Intelligence, Interests, and Manifest Anxiety* (Athens: University of Georgia, College of Education, 1962), pp. 1–2.

89

When a child first enters school he brings a self-concept with him. He was not born with it, but he has been developing it as one part of the process of growing up and will continue to develop and modify it during his years in school. A self-concept develops largely through a child's interactions with people who are important to him. His first feelings about himself are reflections of his parents' feelings about him. Research has shown that there is a significant relation between parents' evaluation and acceptance of their children and the way the children regard themselves and are regarded by their peers.[3] As the child grows, the other members of his family and later his peer group, his teachers, and other members of the community contribute further to the formation of his self-concept. Self-concepts, then, develop to a great extent through the perceptions and evaluations of others: we come to see ourselves as we think others see us.[4]

These self-concepts unfortunately often bear only slight resemblance to a person's actual characteristics. For example many people, by objective standards, have a high academic potential but consider themselves poor students or have been alienated from school even before they entered; whereas others whose academic potential is relatively low consider themselves good students and talk of college or even of graduate work. One of the most significant contributions a teacher can make to the mental health of his pupils is to help each identify the person he really is, to help him make a realistic self-appraisal—recognizing his strong and his weak points —and then to help him remedy the weaknesses.

## The Teacher's Concern with His Pupils' Self-Concepts

There are several reasons why a teacher should be concerned with his pupils' self-concepts, with learning what they are now and attempting to point them in more positive directions.

First, the self-concept, the way a person sees himself, is a good indication of the condition of his mental health. In the process of growing up, a major goal for the child is the development of a sense of personal worth— recognition and respect for himself as an individual. This sense of personal worth, one's self-esteem, is a major aspect of personality organization. Although lack of self-esteem is almost always an indication of stress, tension, and poor mental health, a positive self-concept—as measured by the tools presented below—may not necessarily mean good mental health.

---

[3]Studies relevant to this area are Serot and Teevan, *op. cit.*, and Luszki and Schmuck, *op. cit.*

[4]Chesler and Fox, *op. cit.*, Chapter Two, defines and describes the development of an individual's "role," his learned, customary manner of relating to other persons and to situations in his life. Developing a self-concept and learning to play an integrated set of "roles" are in many ways parallel events in a child's development.

A positive self-concept is generally characteristic of a person who respects and accepts himself and recognizes both his assets and his shortcomings, but occasionally it indicates a person who is highly defensive. Such a person, when asked to describe himself, may overevaluate his assets and minimize his shortcomings, presenting himself as close to "ideal" by denying or suppressing threatening aspects of himself. His self-evaluation is unrealistic, and he may be labeled by other pupils as conceited. But when the self-concept is both positive and realistic, it is one important indication of mental health. A child with this kind of self-concept has confidence and usually is able to utilize his capabilities to a high degree.

Second, the way a person feels about himself is an important determinant of his behavior toward others. The child or adult who holds negative feelings about himself tends to hold negative feelings toward others. The child who constantly criticizes and finds fault with others may feel, perhaps subconsciously, that he himself is not much good. The child who likes and respects himself tends to be positive in his attitudes toward others and to get along better with his associates than the child with negative attitudes.

Third, the pupil with a low level of self-esteem in a particular area is likely to consider himself a failure in that area. His probable course of action will be to try to escape. If school self-esteem is low, a pupil is apt to slip into daydreams or misbehave when he is in school and to drop out of school as soon as possible. Through his inappropriate behavior in the classroom and the associates he chooses outside school, he seeks situations and companionships by which he can see himself in a favorable light and thus build his self-esteem. Pupils whose school self-esteem is low, or for whom self-esteem is unrelated to school achievement, are on the road to becoming dropouts unless corrective action is taken.

Fourth, the self-concept is rather easily accessible to normal change and planned alteration. The self-concept is learned, and the teacher and others associated with the child participate in this learning and changing process.[5] Yet studies have shown that the change during school years is often in the wrong direction. A recent study including both middle- and lower-class children was made by Morse, Bloom, and Dunn;[6] it showed that 88 percent of third-graders felt "pretty sure of themselves," but only

---

[5]Martin Deutsch, *Minority Group and Class Status as Related to Social and Personality Factors in Scholastic Achievement* (Monograph No. 2; Ithaca, N.Y.: Society for Applied Anthropology, 1960).

[6]W. C. Morse, R. Bloom, and J. Dunn, *Characteristics of School Classroom Environments over Time* [University School Research Project (U.S. Office of Education Research Grant 04632), School of Education, University of Michigan, Ann Arbor, 1964], pp. 88–89.

66 percent of eleventh-graders showed similar self-confidence. The same study found rather wide self-dissatisfaction. Of the eleventh-grade pupils studied, 44 percent often wished they were someone else, and 25 percent of all the pupils, third- through eleventh-grade, felt that things were "all mixed up" in their lives and had a low opinion of themselves. These findings refer to their lives as a whole, of which school is only a part, but findings regarding school self-esteem suggest that the school is failing to contribute to the development of a positive self-concept. For example, 84 percent of the third-graders were proud of their schoolwork, but only 53 percent of the eleventh-graders had such feelings. In the lower grades 93 percent felt they were doing the best work they could, whereas only 37 percent of the oldest pupils felt that way. The authors state:

> "Regardless of their achievement quotients and the fact that the failures tend to drop out, the pupils who remain in school come to feel that they are doing inadequate work. Again over half of the young pupils say that they are doing as well in school as they would like, but only twenty-two percent of the eleventh-graders feel this way. About forty percent of pupils at all ages often feel upset in school; with regard to achievement, twenty percent say their teacher makes them feel 'not good enough.' And these items stay virtually the same with age. Over forty percent report they often become discouraged in school, and this increases with age from twenty-two to forty-three percent."

The authors conclude:

> "While neither the self-picture nor the school self-esteem is pleasant, the school self appears to be more negative. Whatever else we have done, we have communicated a sense of personal failure to many of our pupils. In general, the longer we have them, the less favorable things seem to be. Findings like these, when viewed in terms of mental health and school dropouts, point to an unfortunate trend, for these are the pupils who have not dropped out of school."

## Measuring Self-Concepts

Teachers may want to know early in the school year how each of their pupils sees himself. Questions such as the following are likely to come to mind.

• Does he think of himself generally in positive or in negative terms?

- Is his self-concept a rather all-inclusive one that is either mostly good or mostly bad, or is there differentiation according to various areas?

An example of the latter is the boy who knows he is good in athletics but recognizes that he has trouble with academic subjects, particularly English, compared to the pupil who overconfidently feels he can do almost anything or the timid one who fears failure in anything he undertakes. A self-concept that shows differentiation between various areas provides the teacher with some guidelines for developing an action program that can attempt to raise the self-esteem by building on and extending the positive aspects. A self-concept that is low in all areas presents the teacher with a more difficult task.

A teacher can often make rather good informal appraisals of his pupils' self-concepts by listening to their talk and observing their behavior in the classroom, with peers on the playground, and in his private talks with them. He can obtain important insights into a pupil's personality by noting whether his comments about others are mostly positive, mostly negative, or in between, and how these compare with the way he presents himself.

Often, however, more tangible and specific measures of self-perceptions are desirable; these can be obtained both directly and indirectly. Tool 20 is an example of a rather direct type of measure. The teacher should supply each pupil with a class roster assigning a number to each member of the class, as was done in Chapter Three.

The teacher can use the results of this instrument by comparing the way a pupil rates himself with the average rating he gives other pupils in the class. Generally a person will rate himself within the range of the ratings he gives others: if he rates most of his classmates between 3 and 6 on the form, one would expect him to rate himself somewhere between 3 and 6. Discrepant ratings of oneself may suggest a problem, particularly if the child shows other indications of an inaccurate self-perception. If a pupil rates himself significantly higher or lower than his peers, possibly indicating an unrealistically positive or a self-depreciating view of himself, the teacher should consult a school psychologist about the validity of the results and the need for any action.

For other perspectives on the way a pupil sees himself, responses on this form might be compared with those on Tool 18, How Satisfied Are They? and Tool 19, How They See Me, in Chapter Six. These instruments measure family or peer influences on a child that may have significant effects on his self-concept.

These responses can be compared, too, with the ratings derived from

## TOOL 20

Date _____

Your number _____

Class _____

MY CLASSMATES

Everyone has some things about him you like and some things about him
you don't like so much.  Some people seem to have more things about
them you like and other people have more things about them you don't
like.

Look at the circles below.  Suppose that each circle stands for a
different kind of person.  Each person has things you like and don't
like.  Circle 1 has all pluses (+) in it.  This stands for a person
who has only things about him you like.  Circle 9 has all minuses (-)
in it.  This stands for a person who has only things about him you
don't like.  The other circles have different numbers of pluses and
minuses.  These circles stand for people who have different amounts of
certain things about them that you like and that you don't like.

For each person in this class, pick the circle that shows the combination of things you like and don't like.  Then put a check (√) for
each person under the circle you choose.  Check just one circle for
each person. . Do this for yourself, too.  There are no right or wrong
answers.

| | 1 | 2 | 3 | 4 | 5 | 6 | 7 | 8 | 9 |
|---|---|---|---|---|---|---|---|---|---|
| | ++++ / ++++ | ++++ / ++++- | ++++ / ++-- | +++- / +--- | ++++ / ---- | ++-- / ---- | ++-- / ---- | +--- / ---- | ---- / ---- |
| Pupil number | | | | | | | | | |
| | | | | | | | | | |
| | | | | | | | | | |
| | | | | | | | | | |
| | | | | | | | | | |
| | | | | | | | | | |
| | | | | | | | | | |
| | | | | | | | | | |
| Myself | | | | | | | | | |
| | | | | | | | | | |

the Sentence-Completion Form, which is discussed in detail in Chapter Nine. On this form three sentence stems—6, 10, and 31—separated by other types of items, relate to a pupil's self-evaluation. This indirect measure of the self-concept gives more qualitative information than Tool 20. The following responses obtained by a sixth-grade teacher suggest the kind of data produced by this test.

Pupil A, a confident, well-poised girl, wrote:
    When I look in the mirror, *I feel satisfied*. Many times I think I am *quite mature for my age*. When I look at other boys and girls and then look at myself, I feel *good because I have so many friends*.

Pupil B, withdrawn, cringing, unsure of himself, wrote:
    When I look in the mirror, *I wonder how anyone could like me*. Many times I think I am *the most backward person in the class*. When I look at other boys and girls and then look at myself, I feel *different and ugly*.

Pupil C fell between these extremes. He wrote:
    When I look in the mirror, *I see if I look all right*. Many times I think I am *not very good in some subjects but good in others*. When I look at other boys and girls and then look at myself, I feel *better than some and not as good as others*.

To get a quantitative score, this teacher graded each positive response as 3 (each of Pupil A's responses), each neutral responses as 2 (each of Pupil C's responses), and the negative responses as 1 (each of Pupil B's responses). Some pupils, of course, were positive on one item and neutral or negative on another. The teacher added the scores for each sentence and divided the total by the number of sentences answered. She called the resulting measure a self-esteem index and used it to help identify the pupils who were high, medium, or low in the way they felt about themselves. Research has shown that there is a rather close relation between such an index, obtained from sentence completions, and the rating obtained from the positive-negative diagrams in Tool 20 in which pupils rate themselves in relation to their classmates.[7]

In addition to the three sentence stems used for such an index, the Sentence-Completion Form in Chapter Nine includes other sentences that give valuable qualitative information about the way pupils see themselves. For example, the stem "If I should fail in school _____" often gives indications of a pupil's feelings of confidence or lack of confidence about

---

[7]Luszki and Schmuck, *op. cit.*

his school endeavors. Stems in that form that are likely to yield useful diagnostic material relating to the self are these:

- If I could be someone else, I_____
- My teacher thinks I am_____
- I am best when_____
- I am happiest when_____
- What I like to do most is_____
- Most of all I want to_____
- I often wish_____

In the test these stems are separated by other stems designed to elicit different kinds of information.

### A Case Study in Analyzing Self-Concepts

The teacher in a sixth-grade classroom studied the self-concepts of her pupils as revealed by the Sentence-Completion Form and Tool 20 and related these findings to other information about them. On the whole, high self-esteem and high achievement in school seemed to have little relation, but an analysis of the class on the basis of sex and the father's occupational level (Chapter Seven) revealed interesting differences. In this particular classroom about two-thirds of the pupils came from families in which the father's occupation required a moderate amount of training or technical skills and abilities (Category II). There were only two pupils whose fathers were in professional or high-level managerial work (Category I); the rest fell into Category III, jobs requiring little or no training or experience. For her analysis the teacher grouped Categories I and II, separating the boys and the girls; she also divided Category III pupils into boys and girls.

A comparison of the data for these four groups revealed interesting differences. Among the girls from the higher occupational levels there was a clear relation between self-esteem and school achievement. In contrast, the boys with the same level of family occupational background were divided equally between high and low self-esteem, but all except one were low achievers. Whether or not they were making appropriate use of their abilities in schoolwork appeared to make no difference in the way they evaluated themselves. Poor school achievement did not appear to lower their self-esteem; what they did in school seemed irrelevant. The teacher concluded that other values took priority over academic achievement in their self-evaluation.

A very different situation was found among the girls coming from families of low-level occupational backgrounds (Category III). All five in the class showed a low level of self-esteem despite the fact that three were achieving at a high level. The boys from similar backgrounds showed a relation between self-esteem and school achievement, following a pattern similar to that of the girls from the higher occupational backgrounds, but there were too few of them in the class for the findings to have much significance.

This analysis was made from the data on the Sentence-Completion Form, since the teacher felt it would give her not only a rating but qualitative material that might make the ratings more meaningful. As a check, however, she compared the self-esteem index obtained from the Sentence-Completion Form with the ratings on Tool 20, considering those persons as high who rated themselves in Categories 1 to 3, medium in Categories 4 to 6, and low in Categories 7 to 9. She found a high level of agreement in the measures coming from the two tools.

These findings raised important questions in the teacher's mind. Was she working selectively with different segments of her classroom group to produce these differences? Particularly, was she working most effectively with the girls who came from a socioeconomic background similiar to her own? Or were such results to be expected in the age group and the different socioeconomic levels with which she was dealing? She was concerned both about the pupils with low self-esteem, for she knew the undesirable effects of a negative self-image on mental health, and about the underachieving pupils with high self-esteem, for she felt that the latter were evidently placing little value on schoolwork.

She first considered the girls whose fathers were in Category III jobs, studying their sentence-completion responses to obtain clues as to how she could help them.

One girl who was slightly above average in intelligence and achieving at a creditable level seemed to regard school very positively except for the expression of some dislike for homework. She said "Most of all I want to *finish school*" and "This school *is like home to me.*" Her opinion of her teacher's attitude toward her was positive: "My teacher thinks I am *smart in working problems.*" But her opinion of herself was negative, as indicated by such responses as "When I look in the mirror, I *think I am ugly*"; "Sometimes I think I am *going to get in trouble*"; "When I look at other boys and girls and then look at myself, I feel *that I don't have things that I think I should have.*" For this girl, school appeared to be one of the brighter aspects of her life. The teacher recognized, however, that giving the girl opportunities to present herself in a favorable light before her classmates might be a supportive step that could enhance her relations with her peers and thereby improve her own self-concept.

For another girl in the same group the problem was more serious.

Although she was of average intelligence, she was achieving at a low level and her attitudes toward school, herself, and her family were all very negative. She said "When I look in the mirror, I *don't see nothing but an ugly messed-up face*" and "When I look at other boys and girls and then look at myself, I feel *like I am not as good as them.*" There were indications, too, of confusion about her own identity, for she said "Sometimes I think *I am adopted but my mom says I am not—but I am not like other kids.*" Her other responses were consistent in indicating feelings of aloneness, inferiority, and depression. A child such as this one has problems beyond those that can be handled by the classroom teacher, and referral was made to a child-guidance clinic.

The teacher was sufficiently familiar with the literature on intergroup relations to realize that it is not unusual for children from an economically and culturally deprived minority to feel inferior. This is caused by many factors over which a teacher has no control, but she determined to do as much as she could within the classroom to put these deprived children in a favorable light and try to raise their level of self-esteem. She had learned through an experience several years previously that when a child is different from the majority or is actually handicapped, his acceptance by his peer group and his own self-esteem may be enhanced by helping the other pupils to understand the difference or the handicap. In that instance a child who had worn leg braces had given the class some under-standing of how the braces worked and why they were necessary, and later told the other pupils how he had learned to use them to walk again. As a result he had become almost a hero in the eyes of his peers rather than a person to be shunned and looked down upon.

Why not try the same general approach to enhance the status of minority-group children? she asked herself. She decided on a dual ap-proach. First, since some of the children came from ethnic minority groups, she would try to place these groups in a favorable light by em-phasizing their contributions and achievements wherever such material could be introduced appropriately into classwork. Second, she would do what she could in the classroom to help these particular pupils appear favorably in the eyes of their peers. She would also make a greater effort to give positive feedback, not only to these girls but to all the pupils with low self-esteem.

As to the low achievement of the boys, which appeared unrelated to self-esteem, the teacher felt a need to learn more about the kinds of things that they valued highly, that were related to their self-esteem and gave them prestige in the eyes of their peers. What values regulated their conduct, perhaps without their being aware of them? What values did their peer group overtly accept? Were the latter congruent or conflicting with the values that the child brought to class and with the teacher's value system? Such questions may never be answered fully in ordinary classroom activity, but to be aware that differences are present is to take a long step forward in understanding the child whose behavior, attitude, or background is somewhat different from that of the majority, or who is a chronic low achiever.

The search for answers challenged the teacher to get more fully into the boys' world and introduce classroom materials and methods relevant to their values. She had heard the boys talking about taking off in a spaceship rather often: if she were to introduce some materials related to space exploration, she might show, indirectly, the education and high-level technical training needed to be an astronaut. Such efforts, she felt, might increase their interest in school and thus help to change values to the point where school achievement would have a more important place in their self-perceptions than it appeared to have at present.

## Other Measurements of Self-Concepts

There are many other ways of studying pupils' self-perceptions. One useful instrument is Tool 21, the Self-Concept Scale, developed by Bledsoe and Garrison.[8]

On this form, 25 of the adjectives indicate positive qualities; 5 are considered negative (lazy, mean, selfish, jealous, bashful). Pupils rate themselves on each of the 30 adjectives and then check each again to show the way they would like to be. The form is scored as follows: For the 25 positive adjectives, a weight of 3 is given for "nearly always," 2 for "about half the time," and 1 for "just now and then." These values are reversed for the five negative adjectives, with a weight of 1 given to "nearly always," and so forth. Totals of the weighted ratings for "This is the way I am" and "This is the way I'd like to be" give a quantitative measure of how positively a pupil sees himself and also of how much discrepancy exists between the way he pictures himself and the way he would like to be.

Other teachers have used lists of descriptive words and phrases; they ask pupils to mark in one way those most like themselves and to mark in a different way those least like themselves. Another method is through the assignment of English compositions such as were described in Chapter Seven. The teacher might ask his pupils to describe the kind of person he is and the kind of person he would like to be, and perhaps the type of work he expects to do. The psychological literature is full of personality and personal inventories, but these are generally more appropriate for use by school counselors and psychologists than by teachers.

---

[8]Bledsoe and Garrison, *op. cit.*, p. 192.

Regardless of the method used to obtain them, pupils' self-perceptions are valuable data for the teacher, for they serve as a guide to the kind of feedback and treatment appropriate to the various pupils in the class. It is

## TOOL 21

---

Date_____

Your number_____

Class_____

### SELF-CONCEPT SCALE

Each of us needs to know more about what we are like.  This form is to help you describe yourself and to describe how you would like to be. There are no right or wrong answers; each person may have different ideas.  Answer these according to your feelings.  It is important for you to give your own honest answers.

Think carefully and check the answer that tells if you are like the word says nearly always, about half the time, or just now and then. In the second column check the answer if you would like to be like the word says nearly always, about half the time, or just now and then.

| THIS IS THE WAY I AM | | | | THIS IS THE WAY I'D LIKE TO BE | | |
|---|---|---|---|---|---|---|
| nearly always | about half the time | just now and then | | nearly always | about half the time | just now and then |
| ____ | ____ | ____ | Friendly | ____ | ____ | ____ |
| ____ | ____ | ____ | Obedient | ____ | ____ | ____ |
| ____ | ____ | ____ | Honest | ____ | ____ | ____ |
| ____ | ____ | ____ | Thoughtful | ____ | ____ | ____ |
| ____ | ____ | ____ | Brave | ____ | ____ | ____ |
| ____ | ____ | ____ | Careful | ____ | ____ | ____ |
| ____ | ____ | ____ | Fair | ____ | ____ | ____ |
| ____ | ____ | ____ | Mean | ____ | ____ | ____ |
| ____ | ____ | ____ | Lazy | ____ | ____ | ____ |
| ____ | ____ | ____ | Truthful | ____ | ____ | ____ |
| ____ | ____ | ____ | Smart | ____ | ____ | ____ |
| ____ | ____ | ____ | Polite | ____ | ____ | ____ |
| ____ | ____ | ____ | Clean | ____ | ____ | ____ |
| ____ | ____ | ____ | Kind | ____ | ____ | ____ |
| ____ | ____ | ____ | Selfish | ____ | ____ | ____ |
| ____ | ____ | ____ | Helpful | ____ | ____ | ____ |
| ____ | ____ | ____ | Good | ____ | ____ | ____ |
| ____ | ____ | ____ | Cooperative | ____ | ____ | ____ |
| ____ | ____ | ____ | Cheerful | ____ | ____ | ____ |
| ____ | ____ | ____ | Jealous | ____ | ____ | ____ |

| | | | | | | |
|---|---|---|---|---|---|---|
| ——— | ——— | ——— | Sincere | ——— | ——— | ——— |
| ——— | ——— | ——— | Studious | ——— | ——— | ——— |
| ——— | ——— | ——— | Loyal | ——— | ——— | ——— |
| ——— | ——— | ——— | Likeable | ——— | ——— | ——— |
| ——— | ——— | ——— | A good sport | ——— | ——— | ——— |
| ——— | ——— | ——— | Useful | ——— | ——— | ——— |
| ——— | ——— | ——— | Dependable | ——— | ——— | ——— |
| ——— | ——— | ——— | Bashful | ——— | ——— | ——— |
| ——— | ——— | ——— | Happy | ——— | ——— | ——— |
| ——— | ——— | ——— | Popular | ——— | ——— | ——— |

of utmost importance for the teacher to create a climate favorable to the development of a healthy concept of the self. In those instances where the teacher finds a pupil to have a highly unrealistic or a very low self-concept, he may find it desirable to refer the child to a school psychologist or a trained school counselor.

This implies that the teacher, too, in order to be able to take a positive view of his pupils as persons, must himself have a realistic, positive self-image. If he feels inadequate or has an unrealistic concept of himself, he will have difficulty evaluating his pupils objectively and is likely to affect their self-concepts adversely.

Positive, realistic self-concepts can be equated with good mental health. The pupil who is mentally healthy feels he is liked, valued, and accepted by his classmates, describes himself in favorable terms, and feels he is a part of the classroom group. His perceptions of the classroom are relatively free from distortion, and he is adequate to meet both the formal learning requirements and the social and psychological demands of the classroom. Such self-perceptions are major goals toward which teachers should strive.

# CHAPTER NINE

# Sentence Completions:
# A Multidimensional Diagnostic Tool[1]

Sentence completions, or incomplete sentences, have been discussed in several earlier chapters. The responses elicited by these open-ended sentences have provided rich and meaningful information about children and their impressions, feelings, and attitudes in many areas of their lives. This information can provide valuable insights into the data derived from other, more direct measurements as well as useful clues to be followed up by observations, conferences, interviews, or other actions.

---

[1]The material in this chapter is based on an extensive study of the literature. For background information on sentence completion tests and reports of relevant research, the reader is referred to the following:

A. A. Dole and F. M. Fletcher, Jr., "Some Principles in the Construction of Incomplete Sentences," *Educational and Psychological Measurement,* 1955, **15,** 101–10.

B. R. Forer, "A Structured Sentence Completion Test," *Journal of Projective Techniques,* 1950, **14,** 15–29.

B. Kimbell, "The Sentence Completion Technique in a Study of Scholastic Underachievement," *Journal of Consulting Psychology,* 1952, **16,** 353–58.

H. Nash, "Incomplete Sentences Tests in Personality Research," *Educational and Psychological Measurement,* 1958, **18,** 569–81.

A. R. Rohde, *The Sentence Completion Method: Its Diagnostic and Clinical Application to Mental Disorders* (New York: Ronald Press 1957).

J. B. Rotter and J. E. Rafferty, *Manual: The Rotter Incomplete Sentences Blank* (New York: Psychological Corp., 1950).

J. M. Sacks and S. Levy, "The Sentence Completion Test," in *Projective Psychology,* eds. L. E. Abt and L. Bellak (New York: Knopf, 1950), pp. 357–402.

I. Wilson, "The Use of a Sentence Completion Test in Differentiating Between Well-Adjusted and Maladjusted Secondary School Pupils," *Journal of Consulting Psychology,* 1949, **13,** 400–402.

A sentence-completion tool is flexible in that it can be of varying length, from about 10 to 50 items for elementary school pupils; it can be designed to tap many areas of life, such as family and home, attitudes toward school and toward self, aspirations, and the like; and the stems can be variously structured according to the teacher's objectives. Some stems give the pupil wide latitude in what he writes, as in "Children _____." or "When I _____." Other stem structures limit responses to a particular area or even a single dimension. The following stem generally elicits characteristics that children value in the classroom peer group: "The kinds of pupils I like most are _____." The two stems discussed in Chapter Seven, "When I talk about school, my mother (father) _____," are also highly structured items, producing responses that can be coded according to the degree of positive-to-negative affect. Were the last two words omitted from each, such controlled evaluation would not be possible.

Experience indicates that the most effective incomplete-sentence form is one using stems that are variously structured and that tap several different areas. Stems parallel in structure or related to one particular area should be scattered throughout the form; if they are close to each other, pupils are likely to repeat the same answer or make stereotyped replies. Language used in the stems must be appropriate to the level of the pupils completing the form. The wording must be unambiguous; it is necessary to be particularly alert to avoid words that have one meaning in standard English and a quite different meaning in slang. Also, the wording should be such that the stem calls for a response that is meaningful and important to the respondent. The two stems "Some of the best (worst) things about this class are _____." are good because the meanings of *best* and *worst* are clear. They are good, also, because *things* allows considerable latitude. An analysis of replies to these stems shows that responses tend to fall into four major categories: teacher, peers, learning, and socioemotional emphasis. Finally, the use of the plural *things* permits the pupil to list as few or as many items in the best and the worst categories as he wishes. Marked differences have been found among classrooms in the total number of best and worst aspects of the class that are listed.

The Sentence-Completion Form presented here as Tool 22 has been used with excellent results in a large number of classrooms from the third to the twelfth grade, for both diagnostic and research purposes.[2] Teachers will generally find it more satisfactory to use this form than to try to

---

[2]The authors are indebted to Dr. Martin Deutsch, director, Institute for Developmental Studies, and professor, department of psychiatry, New York Medical College, for making available the sentence stems used in his research reported in *Minority Group and Class Status as Related to Social and Personality Factors in Scholastic Achievement* (Monograph No. 2; Ithaca, N.Y.: Society for Applied Anthropology, 1960). Ten of the stems he used are included in Tool 22.

develop completely new forms for their particular classrooms. This form might be shortened, however, by the omission of stems that tap areas in which a teacher is not interested. If new stems are added, some pretesting is suggested to avoid two main pitfalls of sentence completions: (1) stems that tend to elicit the same reply from most people and thus fail to discriminate between pupils ("Going to the movies is _____" or "Eating ice cream is _____") and (2) stems in which the stimulus is so vague that the completions contain no common themes or dimensions (the stem "Children _____" given above). When incomplete sentences are used for clinical rather than classroom purposes, a vague stem is often desirable.

## Administering the Tool

Sentence completions are easy to administer in the classroom if the pupils can read and write. Experience with this form indicates that practically all pupils in the fourth grade and many in the third can perform the task satisfactorily if the recommended administration procedure is followed.

A period of from forty-five minutes to an hour should be allowed for administration of the Sentence-Completion Form to elementary school pupils; twenty to thirty minutes is generally ample for pupils at higher levels, even though they tend to write longer and more complex responses. An introduction such as the following is suggested.

> I'm going to give you a paper with a number of sentences that are started but are not finished. You are to finish each sentence to tell how you really feel. What you write is confidential. I want your personal and private answers, for they will help me to understand you better and to understand the class as a whole. Everybody's answers will be different. This is not a test. There are no right or wrong answers. Just write the way you really feel.

Then distribute the forms and have the pupils fill in the identifying information at the top of the page. Continue by reading the instructions on the form and go over the two examples carefully.

If there are pupils who may have difficulty reading the stems, they should be seated where the sentences can be read to them with the least possible disturbance. If a pupil does not understand a sentence stem, work with him individually, repeating the stem and telling him to fill in the rest. Do not suggest any ways in which it might be completed, but if necessary refer back to the examples at the beginning of the form and read them again. Do not use any other examples. If a pupil asks "Is this the right answer?" the reply should be: "Whatever you want to say. Any answer is right if that's the way you feel."

Particularly at the third-grade level, teachers may permit pupils to request help in spelling. It should be made clear, however, that this is not a spelling test and that the only reason for asking for spelling help is to be sure that a reply will be understood. If a pupil cannot write well enough to complete the blank himself, either the teacher or a competent pupil helper can use the blank as an interview schedule and write down the pupil's responses.

Pupils should be seated so as to minimize copying. If copying appears to be going on, say: "I want your personal and private answers. Everybody's answers will be different. This is not a test. There are no right or wrong answers. Just write the way you really feel. Remember, nobody except your teacher will see what you write."

Stems 21 and 27 refer to "my mother," and 16 and 37 to "my father." If a pupil says that he does not have a mother or a father, tell him to cross out the stem and leave the space blank. Make it clear that all other stems should be answered in a way that completes the sentence. It may be necessary to point out that "Don't know" is not an acceptable answer.

## TOOL 22

Date _____

Your number _____

Class _____

### SENTENCE-COMPLETION FORM

On the lines below are some sentences that are started but are not finished. Complete each sentence to tell how you really feel. Let's try an example. Suppose the sentence reads this way:

A. Today I want to _____

_____

To complete this sentence you might write "play ball," "get a good grade," "finish my homework early so I can go to a show," or many, many other things, depending on what you really want. Here's a harder one:

B. Compared with most years, this one _____

_____

To finish this sentence you might write "didn't have as much rain," "was about the same as most years," "was more interesting for me," or many other things to tell how you feel this year was like or different from most years.

Now start with the first sentence below, telling how you really feel.
Do every one.  Be sure to make a whole sentence.  There are no right
or wrong answers.  Each person will end up with a different sentence.
Hand in your paper as soon as you have finished.

1.  Compared with most families, mine _____

_____

2.  I am best when _____

_____

3.  My schoolwork _____

_____

4.  Someday I _____

_____

5.  Studying is _____

_____

6.  Many times I think I am _____

_____

7.  I learn best when _____

_____

8.  If someone makes fun of me, I _____

_____

9.  Mothers should learn that _____

_____

10.  When I look at other boys and girls and then look at myself, I

feel _____

11.  A nice thing about my family _____

_____

12.  Homework is _____

_____

13.  When I grow up, I want to be _____

_____

14.  Some of the best things about this class are _____

_____

15. I get in trouble when _____

_____

16. I wish my father _____

_____

17. Learning out of books is _____

_____

18. If I could be someone else, I _____

_____

19. If only teachers _____

_____

20. When I am by myself _____

_____

21. When I talk about school, my mother _____

_____

22. To keep from getting into a fight, you must _____

_____

23. I am happiest when _____

_____

24. Fathers should learn that _____

_____

25. To get along well in a group, you have to _____

_____

26. I can't learn when _____

_____

27. I wish my mother _____

_____

28. Making friends is hard if _____

_____

29. What I like to do most is _____

30. If I should fail in school _____

31. When I look in the mirror, I _____

32. My family treats me like _____

33. In class, working by myself is _____

34. When I am older _____

35. Some of the worst things about this class are _____

36. A mother is nice when _____

37. When I talk about school, my father _____

38. I get mad when _____

39. Most of all I want to _____

40. A father is nice when _____

41. In class, working with others is _____

42. At home I _____

43. I often wish _____

44. My teacher thinks I am _____

45. If I were a parent, I _____

_____

46. This school _____

_____

## Scoring and Interpretation

Material from the Sentence-Completion Form can be used in several ways. In the hands of the school psychologist or another trained clinician, responses, taken as a whole, can be used in evaluating the overall adjustment of a pupil. The content can be analyzed from the point of view of emotional quality, including such factors as positiveness versus negativeness of attitude and affect, degree of spontaneity or inhibition, intensity of feeling, frankness or evasiveness, and so forth. An analysis of this sort, however, is a job for the skilled and experienced clinician. If a pupil's responses are quite atypical, a teacher may want to discuss them with a person trained in interpreting psychological test material. Used in this way, the form may be seen as a case-finding tool to help identify those pupils who would benefit from guidance services.

### Scoring Principles

The major use of sentence-completion data in the classroom, however, is as the basis for indexes relevant to classroom diagnosis. For this purpose, a cluster of selected stems relating to a particular content area is coded quantitatively. One example is the self-esteem index described in Chapter Eight, in which Stems 6, 10, and 31 are used. Another example is found in Chapter Seven, based on Stems 21 and 37, where positive, neutral, or negative values are assigned to the pupil's perception of his parents' attitudes toward school. In both cases the stems were coded on a three-point scale, with designations of plus (+), neutral (0), and minus (−).

More accurate coding and greater discrimination among pupils is possible if a five-point scale is used. Each response to a particular stem is scored on a scale from 1 to 5. The score represents the weight assigned to a response in terms of its rated positiveness, or adequacy of adjustment.[3]

---

[3]The scoring system used is adapted from Leslie F. Malpass and Forrest B. Tyler, "Validation of the Incomplete Sentences Test of School Adjustment" (23-page unpublished paper, Southern Illinois University, 1961).

Each important variable is rated on a continuum between what is considered a psychologically healthy attitude or relationship and a psychologically unhealthy one. Healthy attitudes are positive, realistic attitudes expressing feelings of liking for people, school, activities, and the like, or interest or participation in these things. An unhealthy attitude is defined as one suggesting hostility, defiance, conflict, overconformity, withdrawal, inadequacy, or the feeling of being disliked or not accepted by others. In general, the better the adjustment a response indicates, the higher the score assigned to it.

For each item, the neutral response is the midpoint on the scale and is scored 3. It is important that this midpoint be kept clearly in mind. There are several types of neutral responses. Those which are purely descriptive, such as "My schoolwork *is arithmetic, English, and history*," or "Learning out of books is *one way of learning*," express neither positive nor negative feeling, hence are considered neutral. Although they might represent a deliberate attempt to be noncommittal or evasive, judgments of this sort fall in the area of the clinical and are beyond the scope of this booklet. Experience with the methods described here has shown that such factors do not invalidate scoring that has been done objectively on the basis of definite scoring criteria, and that a good degree of reliability and validity can be obtained. Such other responses as "My schoolwork *is average*" are more clearly neutral. This indicates neither like nor dislike, good nor bad schoolwork, positive nor negative reaction. A third type of neutral response is the ambivalent, or compound, response, the parts of which approximately balance and thus cancel out each other. The resultant is about neutral, as in "Studying is *sometimes fun, sometimes not fun*." Finally, responses that are essentially a repetition of the stem ("I get mad when *I get mad*" or "I learn best when *I learn*") are generally scored 3.

After the scorer has the midpoint of responses for a particular stem clearly in mind, he must decide whether the response he is scoring is at that midpoint or whether it is in the positive or the negative direction. If it is positive, it will be scored 5 or 4 depending on how strongly positive it is, a score of 5 being the more positive. If it is negative, it will be scored 2 or 1 depending on how strongly negative it is, 1 being the more negative.

*Positive responses* are those indicating positive attitudes toward school, the self, the family, or whatever aspect of the pupil's life is dealt with in that particular sentence stem. Whether a response is scored 5 or 4 depends on the degree of attraction, liking, positive feeling, happiness or satisfaction, hopefulness, or optimism expressed.

Responses scored 5 are those indicating a good feeling toward others, the family, or the self; liking for, or healthy attitudes about, school; interest or participation in school activities; realistic attitudes toward regulations and rules; good interpersonal relations; healthy spontaneity; realistic and positive attitudes toward the future; and the like:

This school *is a lot of fun.*

Homework is *one of the most important things to me. I like homework.*

This school *is something I like to attend.*

Homework is *very helpful to me.*

The first two responses appear somewhat more positive than the other two, but all are positive enough to justify a score of 5. Responses in this category show a feeling of realistic competence, indicate a healthy (but not extreme) outgoingness, or express a feeling of being genuinely liked and not simply because of special abilities or possessions; they show a genuine liking for teachers and peers as people or a real liking for school and schoolwork. Similar responses, but with slight qualifying aspects, are included in this category. Most humor would be scored 5.

Responses scored 4 indicate a general or mild satisfaction with, acceptance of, interest in, or liking for the aspect of the pupil's life covered in the stem. A response scored 4 presumes an acceptable adjustment on the part of the respondent. Positive responses with significant qualifying aspects are also scored 4 if the positive statement is only partially balanced by a negative element: "This school *is fine, except for some of the kids.*" Responses showing respect ("O.K." or "all right") as opposed to liking, and others that are just a little on the positive side of neutral, would fall into this category.

*Neutral responses,* scored 3, are described and illustrated above, but the evasive or noncommital response deserves further mention. A pupil may want to avoid any risk by describing his feeling in a way that says practically nothing. Occasional responses of this sort can be scored 3 and otherwise disregarded, but when a pupil gives a large number of such responses, a special conference with him may prove fruitful. The purpose of such a conference is, first, to try to understand him better as a person and why he needs to be so guarded and cautious and, second, to obtain information about whether his general attitude actually leans in a positive or a negative direction. In such a meeting the teacher might say, for example, "You said 'I learn best when I learn.' Now, can you tell me more about that?" Through such inquiry the teacher may be able to obtain nonneutral responses that will help him in making a better estimation of the pupil's attitudes and classroom adjustment. When such elaborations are made by pupils, the teacher can add them to the form and rescore the items to which they pertain.

**111**

*Negative responses* are those indicating unwholesome or unhealthy attitudes toward school, self, family, peers, or other forces in the pupil's life that thus suggest school or personal maladjustment. Hostility, pessimism, derogation, rebelliousness, lack of success, and nonacceptance are typical of negative responses.

Responses scored 2 represent a general but relatively minor degree of dissatisfaction, distaste, or worry, mild feelings of resentment, and other kinds of negative reactions that do not seem to be deep-seated or overwhelming: "Studying is *usually dull*," and "My schoolwork *isn't much fun*." This category also includes negative comments with minor positive aspects; overconforming behavior; slight to moderate inadequacy or inferiority feelings; achievement solely to please others; and lack of interest or participation in school activities.

Responses scored 1 are those that indicate more serious maladjustment or negative feelings: clear-cut and rather strong feelings of inferiority or inadequacy; dislike for, rebellion against, or relatively intense difficulties with, school, family, peers, and the like; lack of interest or participation in school activities. Also included in this category are responses indicating severe conflict or maladjustment: extremely strong resentment; open hostility or sullenness; marked defeatism and social isolation; feelings of worthlessness; active dislike and opposition to teacher, peers, family, school. The following are some examples.

Studying is *depressing*.
My schoolwork *is crummy*.
My schoolwork *gives me the creeps*.
This school *I hate*.

The last two are more negative than are the first two, but all are sufficiently negative to justify a score of 1.

These definitions of the five-point-scale categories should provide sufficient guidelines for coding those stems which a teacher wishes to use quantitatively. There are, however, a few other scoring considerations.

Most important is the problem of omitted responses or those answered with a question mark or "Don't know." Whenever feasible, it is desirable to return the form for completion of the unanswered items; otherwise they are coded 0 and are not included in the computation of an index, as explained below. Incomplete or fragmentary responses are also scored 0 unless there is enough feeling included in what has been written to permit its positive or negative evaluation according to the degree of feelings expressed.

## Computing an Index

One group of stems, those discussed in Chapter Two relating to a pupil's feelings about school, is particularly useful to code.

3. My schoolwork _____
5. Studying is _____
12. Homework is _____
17. Learning out of books is _____
46. This school _____

When these five stems are coded according to the principles given above, the total score is obtained and divided by the number of stems involved—by 5 if all the stems are answered. This average score value for the group of stems is the School Adjustment Index. The following examples drawn from the sixth-grade class discussed in Chapter Seven are illustrative. The number after each sentence is its score.

Pupil 1 is a boy whose school orientation, as indicated by his replies, was rather positive. He wrote:

| | |
|---|---|
| My schoolwork *is fun so I get all of it done, as much as possible I can.* | 5 |
| Studying is *helpful because you learn something useful to you.* | 5 |
| Homework is *fun but sometimes it is boring.* | 4 |
| Learning out of books is *a good thing to do but when someone explains it I learn more.* | 4 |
| This school *is pretty good, but the one I went to last year was better.* | 2 |
| | 20 |

Pupil 2 was slightly more ambivalent in his feelings about school. His replies suggest that he might profit by some special help from his teacher. His replies provide a good illustration of the importance of using the qualitative as well as the quantitative aspects of sentence completions:

| | |
|---|---|
| My schoolwork *is good, all but arithmetic.* | 4 |
| Studying is *a little hard for me.* | 2 |
| Homework is *all right, but sometimes I don't understand it. Sometimes my Dad don't too.* | 2 |
| Learning out of books is *fun.* | 5 |
| This school *is O.K.* | 4 |
| | 17 |

Pupil 3 presented a quite negative picture:

My schoolwork *is fair but I hate to do book reports and I play too much.*  2

Studying is *boring for me unless someone is helping me.*  2

Homework is *very boring. I hate to stay in the house to do homework.*  1

Learning out of books is *not hard but I could learn more if the teacher told me.*  2

This school *is crappy and I'm leaving it soon.*  1

—

8

The results for these three pupils are as follows:

| Pupil | Total Score | School Adjustment Index |
|-------|-------------|-------------------------|
| 1     | 20          | 4.0                     |
| 2     | 17          | 3.4                     |
| 3     | 8           | 1.6                     |

The teacher could have used the total score for comparative purposes just as well as the index, but since a few pupils did not complete all five sentences, the average score, or "index," was more useful.

When she compared each pupil's School Adjustment Index with his responses on the two stems dealing with parental attitudes toward school, discussed in Chapter Seven, she found that most pupils who thought their parents liked to have them talk about school had a positive attitude toward school.

## Multiple-Choice Sentence Completions

An alternative form of sentence completions that is less time-consuming and easier for the teacher to score is the multiple-choice sentence completion. The teacher can obtain a picture of overall pupil opinions and attitudes on various aspects of school by counting the number of pupils who select each of the different alternatives. This form has been used successfully in the third grade as well as at higher levels.

It will be noted that this form uses only seventeen of the stems contained in the Sentence-Completion Form, and that some of the stems used are presented with two or three sets of alternatives. These choices have been drawn up from the most frequent responses obtained on the free-answer form. A pupil's consistency of attitude will show up in a comparison of responses to such closely related stems as 8, 16, 21, 24, 28, and 30, each of which taps the same area from slightly different points of view.

The content of this suggested multiple-choice form is closely related to school and school activities. The Sentence-Completion Form has a much broader coverage, with stems related to parents and family, future and vocational interests, self-concept and degree of self-satisfaction, conditions for positive self-esteem, and interpersonal relations. It is important for the teacher to consider the area or areas in which he wishes to obtain data and to use the form that is more appropriate, or to modify these forms to suit his particular needs.

## TOOL 23

Date _____

Your number _____

Class _____

### MULTIPLE-CHOICE SENTENCE COMPLETIONS

On this form are some sentences that are started but not finished. Below each sentence that has been started are some different ways that it might be finished. You are to put an X in front of the one that makes the sentence most true for you. There are no right or wrong answers. The way you feel about things is what counts.

Let's try an example. Suppose the sentence reads this way:

Today I want to

___ play ball

___ get a good grade

_X_ go to a movie

Suppose that what you want most today, of the three choices listed, is to go to a movie. To show that this is your choice, you would put an X on the line in front of the words go to a movie, as has been done in the example.

Are there any questions?

Start with the first sentence below and put an X in front of the one ending that makes the sentence most nearly true for you. Do every one. There are no right or wrong answers. This is not a test. What is right for you would not necessarily be right for somebody else. Hand in your paper as soon as you have finished. Remember, complete each sentence with only one X; that is, put an X only in front of the one ending that comes closest to the way you really feel.

1. My schoolwork

___ is a lot of fun

___ is sometimes fun

___ isn't much fun

___ is not fun at all

2. Learning from books is

___ very interesting

___ interesting sometimes

___ sometimes dull

___ very dull and boring

3. Studying is

___ a lot of fun

___ sometimes fun

___ not much fun

___ not fun at all

4. The best thing about this class is

___ the kids in it

___ the things we learn

___ recess

___ the teacher

___ the fun we have in class

5. My schoolwork is

___ very hard

___ sort of hard

___ sort of easy

___ very easy for me

6. I learn best when

___ I work by myself

___ I work with a friend

___ I work in a group

7. If only teachers

___ would make us work harder

___ wouldn't make us work so hard

8. In class, working with others is

___ the best way for me to learn

___ sometimes good, sometimes not

___ not as good as working alone

___ a waste of time for me

9. My schoolwork is

___ very interesting

___ interesting sometimes

___ sometimes dull

___ very dull and boring

10. Learning from books is

___ a good way to learn

___ good, but I can learn more in other ways

___ not a very good way to learn

___ not at all a good way to learn

11. Studying is

___ very dull and boring

___ sometimes dull

___ interesting sometimes

___ very interesting

12. The worst thing about this class is

___ the kids in it

___ the things we have to study

___ the teacher

___ that we almost never have fun

___ that we have to stay in school too long

13. I can't learn much when

___ I work by myself

___ I work with a friend

___ I work in a group

14. If only teachers

___ would tell us just what they want

___ would give us more chance to work things out for ourselves

15. If I should fail in school,

___ I'd try to do better

___ I'd wish I had studied more

___ I'd feel ashamed

___ I'd quit school

16. In class, working with others is

___ not fun at all

___ not much fun

___ sometimes fun

___ a lot of fun

17. Most of all I want to

___ be rich

___ be smart and know a lot

___ have a lot of friends

___ be able to get others to do what I want them to do

18. Homework is

___ very interesting

___ interesting sometimes

___ sometimes dull

___ very dull and boring

19. When I talk about school, my mother

___ doesn't listen

___ sometimes listens

___ listens most of the time

___ is very interested

20. I learn best when

___ the teacher helps me

___ another pupil helps me

___ someone in my family helps me

___ I can work it out for myself

21. In class, working by myself is

___ no fun at all

___ not much fun

___ sometimes fun

___ a lot of fun

22. If I should fail in school,

___ I'd be mad at the teacher

___ I'd be mad at myself

___ I'd say it was tough luck

___ it wouldn't be my fault

23. Studying is

___ very helpful to me

___ helpful if there is not too much

___ not very helpful for me

___ a waste of time for me

24. In class, working by myself is

___ very easy

___ easier than working with others

___ harder than working with others

___ very hard

25. If only teachers

___ would make us behave better

___ would trust us more on our own

26. I am happiest when

___ I'm with a friend

___ I'm with my family at home

___ I'm alone

___ I'm in school

27. Homework is

___ a waste of time

___ not very helpful for me

___ helpful if there is not too much

___ very helpful to me

28. In class, working with others is

___ very hard

___ harder than working by yourself

___ easier than working by yourself

___ very easy

29. When I talk about school, my father

___ is very interested

___ listens most of the time

___ sometimes listens

___ doesn't listen

30.  In class, working by myself is

___ the best way for me to learn

___ sometimes good, sometimes not

___ not as good as working with a group

___ a waste of time

31.  This school

___ is my idea of a good school

___ is O.K. but it could be better

___ isn't very good

___ is pretty bad--I don't like it

73530

**121**

# CHAPTER TEN

# *Planning and Accomplishing Classroom Diagnosis*

The preceding chapters have presented tools that the teacher can use to achieve a fuller understanding of the many different forces that can influence the learning atmosphere of his classroom. The case studies in many of the chapters showed the importance of considering a problem area, but it is necessary to explore further the different ways in which all the tools can be coordinated to become an integral part of a broad, year-round program of classroom analysis and problem solving.

Before proceeding, a further caution: A teacher who is intrigued by the potential of these tools should remember that any sequence or package of tools that he sets up will be effective only as (1) it reflects his careful planning of the entire problem-solving sequence in light of the realities of his classroom and teaching situation and (2) he remains sensitive and flexible in his responses to each new set of data and to the implications it contains. The teacher should also realize that these diagnostic instruments are only tools, not ends in themselves, and that there must be constant evaluation of their effects on the pupils and their effectiveness in serving educational aims. A general approach such as that suggested in *Problem Solving to Improve Classroom Learning* should be valuable in constructing a classroom program for which these tools would supply vital information. Basic to this approach, however, is the teacher's sensitive and critical awareness of his pupils' needs. Without this sensitivity and understanding, use of the tools could conceivably be more harmful than helpful to the children as individuals and as pupils.

## Scheduling Classroom Diagnosis

Before considering the development of a program appropriate to a particular classroom situation, it may be useful to consider when, during the school year, the various types of instruments might be used most effectively. Certain tools are obviously more appropriate than others for the first week of class. Some information about pupils and their families is crucial early in the year; often it will alert the teacher to potentially negative patterns before the outlines have hardened. It may also alert him to possible personality maladjustment so that remedial action can be started immediately. Other information cannot be obtained until the class has had time to develop structure as a group. The beginning of the fall term is generally a good time to collect information about the forces outside school that may be influencing pupils, including the way they perceive their parents' attitudes toward school. At times a teacher may wish to collect information about the norms or attitudes toward school that the pupils hold when they enter his class, in order to know the attitudes he must work with and perhaps try to redirect. An early evaluation of pupils' self-esteem might provide a similar basis for concrete planning, although the teacher may not then be able to correlate these feelings with actual levels of academic achievement.

The following hypothetical calendar of instruments might be seen as a reservoir that a teacher can draw from in developing a program to meet his particular needs.

Early September: Family background information is collected (Chapter Seven). The teacher appraises forces outside the school that influence the child (Chapter Six). The Sentence-Completion Form is used to obtain a multidimensional view of the pupil (Chapter Nine). In the analysis of these forms, particular attention is given to the data relating to self-esteem (Chapter Eight) and to parental attitudes toward school (Chapter Seven).

Early October: Data on social relations are obtained (Chapter Three). Classroom norms are appraised (Chapter Four).

Late October: A colleague observes during a class period when the teacher tries a unit involving much interaction (Chapter Five). Pupils are asked to react to this unit (Chapter Two).

Mid-November: Self-concepts of pupils are assessed again, this time in a direct manner (Chapter Eight).

Early December: Low-achieving, low-self-esteem pupils are identified and special individual conferences held with them. The teacher reviews tools previously filled out by these students.

Early February: (Conferences with parents are scheduled for the following week.) Pupils' perceptions of parental attitudes toward school are reassessed through readministration of the Sentence-Completion Form (Chapter Seven) and compared with similar data obtained in early September. Other responses on the form are compared with those obtained in September for indications of change in personal and school adjustment.

Mid-March: The general learning climate is assessed (Chapter Two).

Mid-May: Social relations (Chapter Three) and classroom norms (Chapter Four) are assessed again to measure changes during the year.

It is most unlikely that any teacher would use all these tools in a single year. Rather, he would choose from them to meet the needs of the classroom as he sees them.

The desirability of definite but flexible planning cannot be over-stressed. Those tools must be selected and used that will contribute most to the educational and personal development of the pupils. One important area to consider, then, includes the characteristics of the children—age, intelligence, grade level, general maturity, and previous school experiences. Another area includes sociological, socioeconomic, and sociopsychological factors such as parental occupations, cultural background and degree of economic security in the home, and prevailing community attitudes. With these factors as a background, planning must then be based on the problems that the teacher perceives as requiring study. These might derive from various combinations of objective factors. For example, a teacher might be starting to work with children from cultural or socioeconomic groups with which he had had little experience. Or a teacher from a school with a relatively homogeneous, superior group of pupils who is shifted to a group with a wide ability range might feel uncertain as he approaches this new teaching experience.

A program of classroom diagnosis planned at the beginning of the academic year will allow the teacher to utilize the tools at the most opportune times and in the best sequence. This plan, however, should be kept flexible, with a reservoir of techniques for unexpected situations. For instance, if in the course of the year the teacher decided to try a new teaching method or curriculum plan, he might want to evaluate its effectiveness by getting reactions from the pupils. If a pupil or a group of pupils suggested a new classroom practice, he might encourage them to evaluate its effects by using questionnaires they could fill in, score, and analyze.

## Examples of Classroom Diagnosis

**Mrs. Smith,** a fourth-grade teacher, had been told at the end of the term that she was "inheriting a problem class." The third-grade teacher whose class these pupils were leaving told her that most of them lacked interest in school and that quite a number of them, particularly the boys, were real behavior problems and hard to control. During the summer Mrs. Smith thought from time to time about the class she had to face when school opened in the fall and resolved to get the jump on them. She prided herself on being able to make the year in her classroom an interesting and productive experience for her pupils, and she was determined to maintain her good record. As she tried to anticipate the situation that would confront her, she formulated the following questions, based on her talks with the third-grade teacher. If she could obtain answers to these, she would be in a better position to map out her strategy.

1. What are the backgrounds of these pupils? Specifically, what are the educational levels and occupations of the parents? How interested are the parents in their children's schoolwork?

2. What are the children's interests and activities outside school? What people in their lives and what parts of their day are most important to them?

3. How healthy are the children emotionally? Are there problems of personal adjustment that may be interfering with school adjustment?

4. What attitudes do the children have about learning, teachers, and classroom participation? Reports from the third-grade teacher made her feel that antischool attitudes would be quite strong and that active work would be needed to develop healthier feelings about learning.

The third-grade teacher was able to provide some information and to give her impressions of a few children in relation to these questions, but Mrs. Smith felt it would be useful to make a careful study of the entire class.

These, then, were the questions with which she approached the first phase of her program, identifying the problems. They covered all the hypotheses she could think of initially to explain why this was a problem class. To explore them all and make a sound diagnosis and interpretation would take considerable time and effort, but she decided it was worth it.

On the first day of school she told her pupils it would help her to become acquainted with them if they would give her some information about their homes and families and what they did outside school. To obtain this information, she used some of the questions in Chapters Six and Seven. She wanted to know about the educational levels of the parents, whether both parents were in the home, what kind of work the father did, whether the mother worked outside the home, and, if so, what provisions there were for the children after school. She hoped to use information on the education and occupation of the parents in preparing for parent-teacher conferences that year. In the past she had assumed that the parents were more sophisticated about school than they really were.

She also was concerned about the pupils' life after school. The previous year she had not allowed pupils to stay around the classroom after school hours, but the fact that a few had wanted to should have been an indication that these children might be in need of some special assistance. Later she had learned that three of the pupils had to go home to empty houses and feared to do this. Her failure to get the facts was an oversight she would not repeat.

A few days later, to learn more about the personalities of her pupils and their attitudes toward various dimensions of their lives, she gave them as a writing assignment the task of filling out the Sentence-Completion Form (Chapter Nine). This would be a useful supplement to the more structured questionnaire items from Chapters Six and Seven. She saw it also as a good case-finding tool for identifying any pupils about whom a conference with the school counselor might be desirable. The reports of bad behavior she had received suggested to her that there might be one or more children in the class in need of guidance help, whose own maladjustments were adversely affecting the behavior of their classmates.

At the beginning of the second week she used the tools to assess classroom norms (Chapter Four), to learn how the pupils themselves felt and how they thought their classmates felt. She did not ask them to complete the tool How Do You Think Your Teacher Feels? because she had been their teacher for too short a time. What she was trying to obtain here were the attitudes they brought to her class from their previous school experience. As she analyzed these data, she found that nearly half the children personally felt somewhat positive toward school, but that nearly all saw the class as a whole as being quite negative. Here was a double challenge: to change the attitudes of nearly half the class who were anti-school, and also to change the misconception of the entire class that "almost everybody hates school" and the associated belief that to be accepted by his peers one must hold such an attitude, publicly at least.

She spent a lot of time planning classwork and teaching methods to make the material as interesting as possible. To evaluate the pupils' reactions to her efforts, she used Postclass Reactions (Chapter Two) on several occasions but was disappointed to find that pupils persisted in checking the scales at about the midpoint, so that they were of little diagnostic value. Her efforts to involve the pupils actively in the learning process seemed unsuccessful.

Mrs. Smith then decided to ask another teacher to observe the teacher-pupil interaction in her class, using the first observation method presented in Chapter Five. The observer found that nearly half the items on the observation check sheet fell in the Social Behavior and Social Control category, both when Mrs. Smith talked to the whole class and when she talked to individual pupils. The sheet showed, too, that these individual pupils were always boys. When the two teachers discussed the session after class, Mrs. Smith realized that she was expending so much time and effort trying to control some of the boys in the class that she was not doing as good a job of teaching as she had thought.

As they discussed the situation further, Mrs. Smith realized that although she had obtained valuable information about her pupils as individuals, she had almost no information about the way the members of the group felt about and related to each other. She had some reservations about sociometric tests, particularly those asking for negative feelings toward peers, and had been reluctant to use them. But now she realized the importance of identifying the best and least liked as well as the most influential members of the class and ascertaining their attitudes toward learning. If she could discover who were the leaders in the group and the standards they held regarding various aspects of school life, this might give her a key to the problem. She was interested to know particularly whether they were more or less antischool than the group as a whole and the extent to which attitudes varied within this leadership group.

To obtain such information she used a combination of tools from Chapters Three and Four. She limited the sociometric questions to *liking* and *influence*, feeling that a picture of the sociometric structure on these two dimensions would identify the class leaders and reveal any clique structures that might exist. She readministered the tools on classroom norms that she had given at the beginning of the year, both to determine whether there had been any change as a result of experience in her classroom and to obtain current information on the attitudes of class leaders.

As she analyzed this material she felt for the first time that she was making progress. The sociometric data revealed quite a different situation from what she had anticipated. She had seen three of the larger, more disruptive boys as class leaders, children who exerted a lot of influence on their peers. This was not the case. While several other members of the class liked them, five of their classmates listed them as disliked. They also did not rate as high on influence as she had predicted. On the assessment of classroom norms, How This Class Thinks, there was little change between this administration and that at the beginning of the school year, but there was a gratifying shift in the positive direction in response to the questions on the form How Do You Think About These Things? The children's private opinions toward school were becoming more positive, but they were afraid to reveal them to their classmates, perhaps because of the active antagonism of the three boys. On the basis of her testing at the beginning of the year the teacher had decided she should be able to work with these boys herself, but she now decided to have a conference with the school counselor about them, reviewing with him their sentence-completion forms, the background information obtained at the beginning of the year, their school records, and some information about their family situations that the third-grade teacher could supply. The counselor saw all the boys, held several sessions with each, and referred one to a child-guidance clinic. Mrs. Smith regretted she had not taken this action earlier.

In addition to pinpointing this source of trouble in the class, the tools helped her identify several pupils who might have the potentiality for becoming constructive leaders in the class. Although they were not widely liked (no pupils in the class were), they were liked by a few and were not disliked. They were also seen as somewhat influential and their standards were generally proschool. By making them more visible through committee and other special assignments, and by placing them in work groups so that they would come in contact with pupils on whom they might exert a constructive influence, she launched a campaign to change the standards and the sociometric structure of the class. In setting up the work groups she gave particular attention to the choice of assignments that were not too difficult and to which each member of the group could contribute, in the hope that the children could realize the fun and satisfaction of accomplishing something constructive through teamwork.

Role playing was another method she used to build up more positive perceptions of class members, following some of the procedures presented in *Role-Playing Methods in the Classroom*. By careful choice of situations and selection of role players it was possible to expand and change the stereotyped roles of various members of the class. Through these and other methods she was able gradually to build an atmosphere much more conducive to learning than it had been at the beginning of the year, an accomplishment that was confirmed by several more observation periods and by readministration of the Sentence-Completion Form and tools from Chapters Two and Four near the end of the year.

In this example, Mrs. Smith followed quite closely the problem-solving sequence presented in *Problem Solving to Improve Classroom Learning*. Her first step was to identify the specific problem or problems rather than merely to accept the idea that she had a "problem class." On the basis of the advance information she could obtain, she developed a plan for gathering data to diagnose the situation. She made certain interpretations from these data and used them as a basis for developing and carrying out plans for change, particularly her all-out efforts to make the schoolwork interesting and challenging. But she met with little success. She then realized that she might not have done as complete a job as was required in problem identification and diagnosis, so she returned to this phase, looking this time at the dynamics of the class as a group rather than only at the individual members. This gave her new insights and she developed new plans for change. Finally, near the end of the year, she evaluated the changes that had occurred and was gratified to find substantial improvement on the various indicators of school and personal adjustment.

**Mr. Williams** is an example of a teacher who made use of the diagnostic tools in different ways and for different reasons. He taught eighth grade in a racially mixed classroom of a low economic level and found early in the school year that many of the pupils often resisted his suggestions and directions. He had difficulty getting the pupils to complete tasks, to follow directions, or to participate when called upon. In short, Mr. Williams' pupils were resistant to doing the tasks that would lead to effective academic learning.

In order to assess the extent, as well as the source, of this pupil resistance, Mr. Williams administered some sociometric questions from Chapter Three. He asked the pupils to indicate those in the class whom they liked the most, liked less than the others, were most friendly with, and tended to look up to and follow. He also asked them to indicate the pupils who tended to be most cooperative with the teacher, and those who tended to be least cooperative. Along with these questions he chose some on the classroom learning climate from Chapter Two. He asked these questions to see if his pupils viewed the classroom as nonproductive, just as he did.

Upon receiving the pupils' responses, Mr. Williams was somewhat surprised. The results indicated definite antilearning and antischool attitudes on the part of several well-liked and influential students. For instance, he found that some of the pupils who were selected as the most influential and highly liked were also selected as being uncooperative with the teacher. The pupils with group leadership were working against him. Moreover, the most cooperative pupils were ignored or rejected by their peers.

Mr. Williams then decided to give his pupils some of the questions on classroom norms from Chapter Four. He found that most pupils felt it was a bad thing to participate in class and that asking the teacher for help was not encouraged. These social relations and classroom standards ran counter to Mr. Williams' attempts to influence and teach.

One of Mr. Williams' interpretations of the reasons why most of his pupils expressed these feelings was that they usually came to school with antiadult and antischool attitudes. Their parents and their peers did not see the school as a productive, helpful, or pleasant place. In addition, some neighborhood groups fostered activities in opposition to public authorities. Some of his pupils were able to achieve status in the peer group by following their defiant and "courageous" leaders.

Mr. Williams decided to test his theory by using some questions on outside influences on his pupils (Chapter Six) and on parental attitudes toward school (Chapter Seven). He especially wanted to see if his pupils would rate school and teacher low in importance and if they perceived their parents as holding nonsupportive attitudes toward school. His predictions were corroborated by the data.

The teacher then tried to change the situation in his classroom by following two strategies. First, he tried to attract more parents to the classroom and the school. Through their visits he was able to convince some parents of the importance of school. Second, he started a pupil steering committee which would provide peer leadership in the development of more positive standards. He hoped to put classroom leaders in a responsible position of working in cooperation with the teacher instead of against him. He used the sociometric leaders in the first steering committee.

He tried to evaluate his behavior in the steering committee by using interaction analysis. He asked a few of his brighter students to help him collect the data. His major objective was to be as indirect and supportive as possible. The pupils enjoyed helping in this way and felt closer to the teacher because of his interest in his own self-evaluation.

Mr. Williams also wanted to do special work with students with low self-esteem. He used the Sentence-Completion Form in order to assess the self-esteem of each of his pupils. He found that some of the most aggressive and uncooperative youngsters had the lowest self-esteem scores. With these pupils, he tried to find school assignments that would bring them a feeling of accomplishment and satisfaction.

Toward the end of the school year Mr. Williams once again gave social relations questions and those on classroom norms. He wanted to see if any changes had taken place other than those obvious to him in his more positive relations with pupils. He was gratified to find that the liking and influence patterns were quite diffused, whereas previously these choices had been concentrated on only a few pupils. He was pleased to find also that the previously uncooperative pupils were much more cooperative. Questions on norms also indicated improvement: the pupils felt that participation in classroom activities was a good thing and that asking for help from the teacher was O.K.

**Miss Miller,** who taught high school social studies in an upper-middle-class neighborhood, was concerned that her students were failing to take initiative in their learning tasks, although the class was generally above average in academic potential. Miss Miller, in contrast to Mrs. Smith and Mr. Williams, used only a few tools for a much more narrowly circumscribed classroom problem. She found that most classroom discussion centered on topics and issues she proposed. Students seemed to understand the factual material she presented, but they were not excited or really interested in learning. Although she tried to stimulate students, they seldom introduced new and different topics into the classroom discussion or related their interests and concerns to any of the classroom work.

Miss Miller decided to administer the items on clues to a good and bad day in the classroom (Chapter Two). Moreover, she constructed some of her own questions patterned after the "direct" questions in Chapter Two on student interests and attitudes about schoolwork. She also administered questions on group norms from Chapter Four. Through the use of these questionnaires she found that the students thought that all classroom planning should be the task of the teacher and that the proper role of the student is the passive absorption of content. The students depended upon her to initiate and maintain their interest in academic tasks. Furthermore, they generally felt quite negatively about learning tasks. Essentially, her problem was a lack of student motivation to take the initiative in learning.

Miss Miller asked a colleague to visit the class for purposes of observation. They decided to use both the Classroom Observation form and interaction analysis. After a three-day training period and about a week's observation of fifty minutes per day, the two teachers had a conference in which they went over the results. It became obvious that Miss Miller was mostly talking in a neutral way to the whole class about social studies content and that most of her interaction with the students was direct: she was creating disinterest and dependency. Next she and her colleague held another conference in which Miss Miller set the objectives of involving individuals more in classroom discussion and of being more indirect and supportive toward her students. Subsequently more observations were made by Miss Miller's friend and more feedback sessions were held between the two.

Later in the year Miss Miller again administered questions on the learning climate and classroom norms. She found that improvements had been made. She traced these back to changes in her own teaching style and interaction with the students.

3-17-1